BRAVE
NEW
GIRLS

This book is the property of

_____

A Brave New Girl

To Rosemary and Mariel
The sunshine of my life

ACKNOWLEDGMENTS

Thank you to my dear family and friends for all your love and support. Special thanks to my agent, Connie Goddard, for believing in my work. To Beth Hatlen, for her delightful illustrations, which add such a lively touch. And to Jessica Thoreson, my editor, for bringing the pages to life with her dedicated work, great sense of humor, and boundless energy.

Contents

Published by Fairview Press, 2450 Riverside Avenue South, Minneapolis, MN 55454.

Library of Congress Cataloging-in-Publication Data

Gadeberg, Jeanette, 1953–
    Brave new girls: creative ideas to help girls be confident, healthy, & happy / Jeanette Gadeberg/
        p. cm.
    ISBN 1-57749-049-5 (alk. paper)
    1. Girls--Life skills guides--Juvenile literature.   2. Girls--Attitudes--Juvenile literature.   3. Girls--Psychology--Juvenile literature. I. Title.
HQ777.G33 1997
646.7'0083--dc21
                                                                    97-15838
                                                                    CIP
                                                                    AC

FIRST EDITION
First Printing: September 1997

Printed in the United States of America
01 00 99 98 97   7 6 5 4 3 2 1

Cover design: Laurie Duren
Illustrations: Beth Hatlen

Publisher's Note: Fairview Press publishes books and other materials related to the subjects of social and family issues. Its publications, including *Brave New Girls*, do not necessarily reflect the philosophy of the Fairview Health System or its treatment programs.

For a free current catalog of Fairview Press titles, please call this toll-free number: 1-800-544-8207.

brave new girls

*Creative Ideas to Help Girls Be
Confident, Healthy, & Happy*

Jeanette Gadeberg

Fairview Press
Minneapolis

Introduction

My dream is for you to like yourself and feel really good about who you are. I want you to be able to look the world squarely in the eyes and say what you think and what you want, and be willing to work hard to make this world a better place for everyone. After reading this book, you can say, "I like myself a lot, thank you very much!"

Grab your pencils, girls! *Brave New Girls* is your book. Take a minute to fill in some hot information about who you really are.

Totally ME!

My whole, complete, real name is:

But everybody calls me:

Most of the time I feel:

But then other times I feel:

I'm kind of
_____wild and crazy
_____sweet and shy
_____totally into sports
_____mysterious—nobody really knows who I am
_____better words to describe me are:

Mystery Girl

Other people think I'm:

My biggest dream is to:

Truth? I'm totally scared of:

Something nobody knows about me is:

WATCH OUT, WORLD—
HERE I COME!

The thing I do that drives everybody crazy is:

Sometimes when I'm seriously bored I:

When I'm out of the house, I just love to:

I'm good at playing:

My biggest dream is to:

I am totally, seriously, fabulously good at:

My Brilliant Self

My favorite subject is:

My favorite time of day at school is:

My absolute best subject is:

My best score this year was in:

I think it's okay for girls to be smart and show it:

_____ Yes _____ No   WHY?

Absolute Favorites

My totally favorite snack is:

My all-time favorite stuffed animal is:

When I'm by myself, my favorite thing to do is:

My favorite season is:

I like to go to bed at   o'clock

                                        and sleep until

I would like to take a trip to:

Someday I'm going to:

Take a good, long look at your answers. What do they say about you? Do you see any patterns? Maybe it looks like you are an energetic, athletic, high-spirited girl. Maybe your answers show a girl who is quieter, thoughtful, easy-going, and even a little moody.

Read over your answers one more time and then make a statement about yourself based on what you just read. For example:

My name is Melissa and I'm an independent girl who likes to try things out for myself. I'm going to make a huge splash in the world with my talent and brains!

Or:

My name is Courtney and I'm a major sports fan. I can do just about anything I put my mind to and I know I'm going to go to the Olympics someday.

YOUR TURN!

READY,

SET,

GO!

Chapter 1

SMART & Sassy!

What Do I Think?

Check it out! "X" marks the statements that best describe the kind of girl you are and what you think:

_____ 1. I don't really give a hoot what others think. I do things my own way.

_____ 2. I'm not really sure what I think.

_____ 3. If someone really wants to do something, I'll just go along. What's the problem?

_____ 4. I am not, I repeat, NOT going to go to school dressed in something stupid-looking, even if it is "costume day."

_____ 5. What girl in her right mind would keep quiet when something really unfair is happening?

_____ 6. I'd rather just keep the peace and not make much noise about anything.

_____ 7. I'd rather wait for my friends to call me. I don't really like calling someone up and asking them to do something with me.

_____ 8. Me? I love to be on the stage.

_____ 9. I'd sooner eat a bug than give a presentation out loud in front of the whole class.

_____ 10. I always make sure I get my turn to do something fun.

_____ 11. I've got lots of good ideas and try to get my friends to go along with me.

_____ 12. I hope and pray that the teacher calls on someone besides me.

_____ 13. I think grown-ups should definitely listen to kids!

_____ 14. I don't really care if someone else wants to be in charge. It's easier to just follow along.

_____ 15. Don't be surprised if I become the first woman President of the United States of America!

A Girl on the Go

If you put a checkmark next to questions 1, 4, 5, 8, 10, 11, 13, or 15, you may prefer to take the lead, make a little noise, and let the world know you're here! You come up with great ideas and want others to go along with them. You don't sit still for injustices and you let your opinion be known. It's important to remember to let others have their way sometimes, too, and to listen to the ideas and opinions of others.

A Girl Who is Quieter Around the Edges

If you put a checkmark next to questions 2, 3, 6, 7, 9, 12, or 14, you may feel more comfortable with others in the lead. You're happy to follow along and enjoy the scenery. Sometimes you don't react right away and you tend to take your time rather than rush into something you're not too sure about. You may want to experiment with taking the lead from time to time, and remember that your ideas and opinions are as valuable as anyone else's.

If you find that your answers were "a little of this and a little of that" (a mix, in other words), what does this say about you? It says you have a wonderful combination of personality traits. You can step forward and be a leader at times, and yet you are able to see the importance of sometimes following along. You can speak up and say what you need to say and also be a good listener. You will probably want to continue developing both of these personality traits to design your own personal style.

Girls, Your Opinion Counts

Alyssa's class was working on a huge project that was going to last at least three weeks. Everyone had their own part to do, but the group had to work out ways to handle problems that came up. Alyssa was in a group with four of her best friends and Becca, a girl who got on her nerves just by walking into the room. It wasn't long until Becca and Alyssa were glaring at each other in disagreement. Becca tended to voice her opinion loudly, and that intimidated Alyssa, who backed off and let Becca have her way, even though she really didn't agree with Becca's idea. Inside, Alyssa was furious, but she didn't know what to do. She wondered how she could ever finish this project with Becca around, but she didn't want to get in trouble or get a lousy grade, either.

Have you ever felt like your opinion just disappeared because someone else was louder or stronger? What can you or Alyssa do to fix this?

Important opinions. First of all, know that your opinions, beliefs, values, and ideas are just as important as anyone else's.

Different opinions. It's absolutely cool that your opinions are different from someone else's. Always having the exact same opinion as everyone else can be so boring!

Find your voice. Figure out what you think or want in your head, then turn it into words—

—AND SAY IT RIGHT OUT LOUD!

It's okay to ask for help. You don't have to try to solve everything by yourself. Ask your teacher to help you and your group work things out. Teachers are not just there to teach what's in the book, they can teach you how to be a friend, get along, and solve all kinds of problems.

Work toward a compromise. A compromise is agreeing to meet in the middle. You give a little, and your friend gives a little. You get something you want, and someone else gets some of what they want. It usually works like a charm.

Here's what Alyssa and Becca did:

1. First, they got everyone involved. They decided to make decisions as a group and not let any one person be totally in charge. That helped a lot.

2. Next, they explained their problems and disagreements to their teacher, Ms. Sanchez. (Little did they realize that Ms. Sanchez had put them together for this very reason! She wanted the girls to learn to find ways to get along and work together.) Ms. Sanchez was more than willing to help the girls talk through their disagreements and problem-solve with her. She helped guide them toward solutions that worked for them. Having a teacher involved helped both girls calm down and think more clearly.

3. They decided to divide tasks among each girl in the group. Each girl was responsible for her own piece and nobody got in anyone's way. As the project began to come together, the girls each added their own individual pieces to make one glorious whole project, earning them a strong A–!

Think about it. There are lots of fun ways to make your opinion known. You can shout it out, sing it out, dance it out, write it out, and more. Of course, it takes tons of courage to say what you think, especially if everyone else thinks something different. Even if you don't feel super-gutsy all the time, you can work hard to "find your voice" and make your opinion known.

Take a look at this list of what making your opinion known really is and what it isn't:

MAKING MY OPINION KNOWN

Is:	**Is not:**
Being in charge of my life.	Being a snot, bully, or obnoxious.
Listening to others, but stating my opinion clearly and firmly.	Dumping my opinion on everyone, no matter what!
Being open to compromise.	My way or no way!
Speaking up. Letting others know my ideas or suggestions.	Hogging the conversation.

MAKING MY OPINION KNOWN

Is:	Is NOT:
Sitting up in front.	Hiding out. Being a doormat. Being quiet as a mouse.
Being brave enough to try out an answer, even if it's wrong.	Clamming up, even when I think I might know the answer.
Keeping a positive attitude.	Complaining and making a big deal out of it when things go wrong.

Making Really Good Choices

I'm in charge here!

Remember the last time you made a bad decision? I mean a really, really dumb choice, the kind that makes you groan just thinking about it? You probably thought it was a pretty good idea at the time, but afterward you could have just kicked yourself. Maybe you ended up feeling incredibly embarrassed and wished you could have crawled inside a paper bag and stayed there for the rest of your life. Anyway, you lived through it and came out all in one piece—embarrassed, sorry, mad, with a few scrapes and bruises, but alive to talk about it.

So, how does a girl go about making her own choices and end up with good results? Consider Abby and Courtney:

Abby was not one to sit around and wait for anyone else's help. In fact, bless her heart, she tended to just barge ahead with whatever idea fluttered across her brain. Sometimes this worked just fine. Abby jumped into her projects with enthusiasm and a ton of natural energy. She was a real go-getter, and her friends loved to join in with whatever idea Abby had up her sleeve, because it usually meant something fun was about to happen.

Abby always managed to be doing about ten different things at once. Most of the time she got everything finished in the nick of time, although she usually left a huge mess behind her wherever she went. (Who had time to clean up? There were always new ideas and projects to tackle.)

But there was a downside to Abby's roaring-through-life approach. She never seemed to think anything through before she got started. If she had an idea, she was off and running before she could think about what might happen next.

The problem? Abby was always getting herself into hot water. She was in such a hurry that she was often hurting other people's feelings, as well as making more mistakes than she could ever correct or clean up. She had a good time, but the results of her actions were never quite what she planned. She couldn't understand why her great ideas and projects never worked out as well as she expected.

Courtney, on the other hand, lived in a world of daydreams and wishes. She had a hard time making up her mind about what to do, so she usually ended up doing nothing or waiting until it was too late and then felt terribly disappointed about having missed a fun time. It was hard for Courtney to take the lead, call up friends, and suggest fun things to do. She preferred to wait around and see if someone called her or someone else had a good idea. She didn't like to be in charge of anything because it felt like way too much responsibility. She hated the idea of being different or sticking her neck out with new ideas or opinions. If everyone decided to wear jean overalls, then that's what Courtney wore. If everyone decided to watch a certain TV show on Tuesdays, then so did she. She detested making up her own mind. She wanted to be brave and speak out sometimes, but she felt miserable at the thought of looking stupid or sounding dumb. So she just kept quiet and went along with the crowd.

The problem? Sometimes her group of friends did things she didn't really want to do—or couldn't afford to do, anyway. Then she felt left out and didn't know how to put her own ideas into action. She never practiced stating her own opinion or marching off in the direction she wanted to go whether or not everyone else came with her. In short, Courtney didn't like to do anything on her own. She always wanted to follow everyone else. Without the crowd, she felt lost and unsure of herself.

WHAT ABOUT YOU?

Do you seem to close your eyes and jump into any decision that seems like a great idea at the time? Do you keep making the same sorry choices that get you into trouble over and over? Or do you freeze and get stuck not knowing what to do? What's *your* style?

Write down the last really dumb decision you made, the one that makes you scrunch up your nose and eyes just thinking about it:

Now write down the last really great decision you made, the one that makes you grin from ear to ear just remembering your brilliant move:

What made the one choice really disgusting and the other one really super?

Remember that it's perfectly okay to make odd and weird choices sometimes, choices that are different from your friends.

Think about some of the decisions you made in the past. How did they turn out? If they didn't turn out so hot, what could you have done instead? List two things you could have done that may have made things turn out differently:

1.

2.

Let yourself slow down just long enough to think through how your decision is going to affect the future. For example, will you be using up all your allowance money so you won't have any left for the last two weeks of the month? Will you be totally exhausted and not able to stay awake to study for your science test if you stay up all night at the slumber party? Will your big sister have a screaming fit if you wear her sweater without asking her? Think ahead and save yourself some grief.

GETTING UNSTUCK

Don't get too freaked out about what might happen if you make your own decisions and they don't always turn out very well. You can learn a lot from your mistakes, even though you end up feeling like a doorknob. What's one thing you learned from your last really doofy mistake?

Remember that your parents and teachers can help you untangle any really big mess you make. Always try to look back over what you did and figure out what went wrong, so you can steer clear of that path next time. Make a few small choices and decisions for practice. Record them here and see how they turn out.

My latest decision:

How I felt about it after I made it:

How things actually turned out a day (or an hour or a week) later:

Would I make that same decision again?

Yes   **No**

Why or why not?

Always try to think through at least the next step of your plan. Ask yourself what will happen next. Then what will happen after that?

Courage

Making a decision that is different from your friends can be really hard. You want to feel like you belong and you don't want to be left out. Doing something different can be scary.

Here's a decision I would secretly like to make but I'm afraid nobody would agree with me:

Are you afraid that if you make your own decisions your friends will get mad and think you're a selfish snot?

Yes   **No**

Do you go along with whatever anyone else wants just to avoid a possible fight or hurt feelings?

Yes   **No**

You are not, I repeat NOT, being selfish if you state your opinion and follow your own heart and mind! Be brave—do what you know is right for you.

STUBBORNNESS

Do you sometimes dig in your heels, plug your ears, and refuse to listen to anyone else? Stubbornness can drive everyone crazy, but it's not all bad. Stubbornness helps you stand firm when the going gets tough. Stubbornness can also be the push that keeps you going when everyone else wimps out on you, leaving you alone to act on an important goal you have, such as learning to ice skate or play the violin, hitting a homerun, or entering your project in the science fair.

> Don't get so stubborn that you can't see or hear other ideas or solutions to your problem. In the spirit of teamwork, play around with the ideas and choices of others to see how they would work.

LACK OF CONFIDENCE

Hey, don't forget to give yourself credit for your good ideas and creative thinking. Your idea doesn't have to be perfect or practical to be good. Let your creative juices flow and never slam the door of your mind shut!

Self-value

Be sure you pay attention to what you value and take action on your dreams. Don't sit around and put off making great decisions for yourself.

STANDING FIRM

Jena couldn't believe how hard it was to get along with Rita. She didn't see how anybody could possibly like Rita (what a bossy cow!), and now Jena was stuck working with her on a science project. "Great," mumbled Jena, "this is going to be a total disaster. Every time we try to work together on a project it just ends up in one big fat fight."

Jena could see it all now; she would make a suggestion and Rita would make a face and say, "No way." Her teacher, Ms. Anton, suggested they "compromise," each making suggestions and each giving a little and taking a little. Jena rolled her eyes. "I tried that, but Rita's too stubborn to give, she just wants to get and have everything go her way. I can't work with her; nobody can, she's too bossy!" Jena slammed her locker shut, stomped off, and headed for the lunchroom. What now?

It's natural for Jena—and for you—to have opinions that are different from those of your friends. It can be really hard when what you think or want is totally different from someone else, especially when you think you're right.

Jena needs to give herself time to chill out; she's too mad right now to think creatively or come up with good ideas about how to fix this mess or say anything pleasant to Rita. Jena needs to take a quick look in the mirror and accept her own stubbornness. She's pretty fluffed up right now, too, so she's not exactly easy to get along with, either.

Being stubborn isn't all that bad, but sometimes it gets in the way and you have to change stubborn behavior into compromising or cooperative behavior. That's hard when you feel you're right and the other person is totally at fault.

How do you know if it's time to try to compromise? How do you know if you're being a total doormat and letting someone walk all over you, or if it's time to put the nasty words and faces away and meet in the middle?

Here's a list to help you figure out the difference between when to give in a little and go along with what others want and when it's time to stand firm. Think about these things the next time you're in a sticky situation.

WHEN TO COMPROMISE	WHEN TO STAND FIRM
When you both want to use the computer at the same time.	When someone wants to use your answers to cheat on a test.
When you want to see a different movie than your friend does.	When someone wants you to do something that makes you feel uncomfortable.
When you want extra time on the telephone or in the bathroom.	When someone wants you to try something disgusting, like smoking or drugs.
When you're working as a team on a school project.	When someone tries to talk you into something you know is bad, wrong, or will get you in major trouble.
When you know it's important to be open to new ideas.	When you feel really, really, strongly about something.

Dear Brave New Girl:

I really like my friend April. She's fun to be with and always acts sort of nuts—which I really like. But she usually doesn't want to include other girls when we do stuff. She just wants to hang out with me. Sometimes she even laughs at kids when they make a mistake in class, or aren't very coordinated in gym. Besides, she always wants us to do what she wants and doesn't seem to want to share. Like I said, I really like her, but I feel kind of stuck with her. Do you know what I mean? What can I do?

> SIGNED,
> FEELING STUCK

Dear Feeling Stuck:

I see your problem. You wish your friend would be a little more open-minded and able to "share," and that means sharing you as a friend, too. You also seem pretty uncomfortable with how she treats other kids. Of course you can't change her behavior, but you can make some good decisions for yourself about how you want to treat others. Treating others disrespectfully is really an ugly behavior that many people use in hopes of making themselves look better. It never works. They just make themselves look bad. As the saying goes, "Anyone who tries to paint the sky just ends up covered with paint." I think that means that your friend just ends up looking bad when she treats others bad. What can you do? Here's a few ideas:

> Use the "inclusion rule"— insist that everyone has a chance to hang out together. Nobody gets left out . . . nobody.

> Refuse to laugh along with her if she teases people because they are different or make a mistake. Point out to her that you think she's acting mean.

The world is full to bursting with other people, each one unique and different. Maybe April doesn't know how to appreciate people who are different. Show your friend how much you enjoy each person for who she or he is.

If you like different kinds of people and activities, other kids will really like you and you will be a welcome addition to any group. Maybe April will see how much you are liked and will begin to change her behavior.

Developing a Positive Attitude

Isn't it fun to be around girls who are happy, light-hearted, and cheerful? Of course everyone has problems, including you. Not everything goes right and some days are really the pits. But remember that you are in charge of your attitude. You get to decide how to react to any problems that come along. If you decide to roll over and croak, that's your business. But you can always decide instead to ask for help and break your problem down into tiny pieces that you can solve one at a time. You can decide to have hope and faith that life will turn out in the best way, which will give you a healthy spurt of energy to tackle the day.

Self-Talk

Do you ever talk to yourself when you think no one's around? You know, sometimes you stand in front of the mirror and carry on a perfectly wonderful conversation with—well, yourself. I suggest having a good conversation with yourself at least once a day. The only thing that might worry me is what you say to yourself. Do you give yourself a lot of mumbling, negative messages? Do you tell yourself what a dope you are, how stupid your answer was, or how bad you were in gym today?

STOP!  **NO MORE NEGATIVE GARBAGE TALK FOR THIS GIRL!**

Positive Affirmations

You are now going to learn how to be your own best friend. Here's how. Affirmations are short little messages you give yourself throughout the day. You can write them out on little pieces of paper and stick them up on your bathroom mirror or bulletin board. Most important is to say them to yourself every single day, no matter what. And say them out loud! Yup, right out loud, looking in the mirror. Why on earth would you want to do this weird thing? Because (get this) what you think about yourself and what you tell yourself are exactly what you will become. This is called self-fulfilling prophecy, which means you can predict exactly what you will become. Here are some affirmations to get you started.

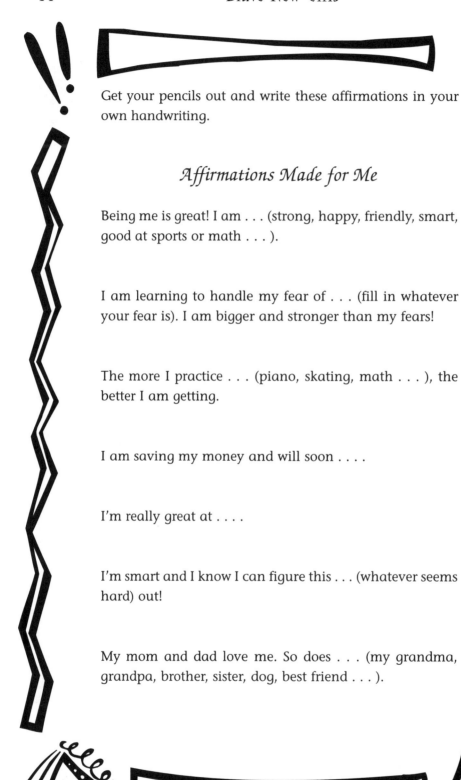

Get your pencils out and write these affirmations in your own handwriting.

Affirmations Made for Me

Being me is great! I am . . . (strong, happy, friendly, smart, good at sports or math . . .).

I am learning to handle my fear of . . . (fill in whatever your fear is). I am bigger and stronger than my fears!

The more I practice . . . (piano, skating, math . . .), the better I am getting.

I am saving my money and will soon . . . .

I'm really great at . . . .

I'm smart and I know I can figure this . . . (whatever seems hard) out!

My mom and dad love me. So does . . . (my grandma, grandpa, brother, sister, dog, best friend . . .).

I'm safe. It's okay to . . . (go to sleep in the dark, go to camp, stay home alone).

My body looks just great. I like my hair and how I look.

Good start! Now promise to practice these out loud every single day to help build your self-confidence and good decision making skills. Also, make up some of your own:

ACTION PLAN!
My Story

Make "her-story"! Start a journal or diary with you as the star. You can use a computer, if you have one, or just get yourself a neat notebook. Write down everything you can think of, such as how you feel about a fun activity you did, a great weekend you spent with friends, or a favorite holiday activity. Keep your writings in a safe and special place. Let your family know about your project so your parents can help you keep track of your papers.

The goal? When you're about to graduate from high school, gather your writings and take them to a bookbinding company who will "publish" them in a real book, with a hard cover and gold lettering for the title of your choosing. You can have them print one or a hundred copies—as many as you want. You will have your very own life story in a real book that you can read over and over for the rest of your life! Definitely a good idea.

WORD FIND

FAIR	**OPEN MINDED**
DECISIONS	**HAPPY**
OPINION	**COMPROMISE**
HERSTORY	**AFFIRMATIONS**
VOICE	**SPEAK UP**
CHOICES	**COURAGE**

```
R  H  I  F  A  H  A  P  P  Y  E  X
E  S  I  M  O  R  P  M  O  C  G  P
V  S  P  E  A  K  U  P  G  D  A  O
O  P  I  N  I  O  N  F  A  I  R  W
I  D  E  C  I  S  I  O  N  S  U  A
C  Y  R  O  T  S  R  E  H  V  O  T
E  S  E  C  I  O  H  C  B  E  C  A
D  D  E  D  N  I  M  N  E  P  O  Q
S  N  O  I  T  A  M  R  I  F  F  A
```

Chapter 2

ME, Myself, & I

Millions of Feelings

Dear Brave New Girl:

I'm eleven years old and in the sixth grade. I don't understand why sometimes my feelings get so mixed up. I never used to feel like this. One minute I'm happy, and then all of a sudden for no reason I feel so crabby that I cry or yell at everybody. I really do love my family and friends, so why do my feelings change so much? And why do I act like this when I really don't even mean to? What's going on?

SIGNED,
LOTS OF FEELINGS

Dear Lots of Feelings:

Feelings can be confusing. Sometimes they seem to come out of nowhere and catch you totally by surprise. Even a year or so ago, this didn't seem to happen, and now you're never sure how you're going to feel. Here are some things you can do to help understand your moods:

Remember, it's okay to have your feelings. They're part of who you are. Identifying what you're feeling is the first step in dealing with how you feel.

Next, "listen" to your feelings. Often your feelings are trying to tell you something—you're tired, your feelings are hurt, you're angry, you're upset because things didn't turn out the way you thought they would, etc.

Share your feelings with someone you trust. Sharing your feelings can lighten your load. If you share your happy feelings, they seem to make things even happier. When you share your sad and angry feelings, they seem to get smaller or even disappear.

Get to know all your different feelings and try to learn what makes them happen. When you get a strong feeling or change of mood, stop and ask yourself, "What just happened to make me feel this way?" or "What am I thinking or worrying about to make this feeling happen?" For instance, everything's going along just fine and then you hear that your friend is having a party and you didn't get invited. Suddenly you feel sad, depressed, lonely, and left out. Or sometimes what we tell ourselves in our own heads makes our feelings change. You might be feeling just great—until you remember that you're getting your science test back today. Suddenly you freak out because you think you failed it, but you're not really sure.

As you grow and change, your feelings change, too. You might not feel like doing the same things you used to do with your friends and family. You might want more time in your room or outside the house. You want more independence, but you want to feel safe and loved, too. Read on for more info on your new and "strange" feelings.

Changing Feelings

Feelings are an interesting part of life, but they sure can be confusing! One minute you're feeling really great, happy and excited, and the next you're in

tears or really mad at someone. Or one minute you feel confident, happy and on top of the world, and the next you feel totally stupid and ugly. You wonder if you're completely nuts—which one is the real you?

First off, all your feelings are a part of you. It's perfectly normal to be feeling a whole bunch of completely different feelings, sometimes all at the same time! Sometimes your feelings change within minutes, and sometimes they build up over time until they are almost too big to handle. Some feelings will be new. Others will be feelings you've had before, but suddenly they're really intense. Sometimes your feelings are so strong that you think you might explode.

When you were younger, feelings seemed to go away more quickly and easily. A few years ago, you probably felt pretty good most of the time, except when you were really upset or angry or hurt. Now, your feelings bounce around all day long.

Why Do I Feel Like This?

It can be hard to figure out why you feel the way you do when your feelings change so much and so quickly. Here are some ideas to consider.

All of a sudden, you are beginning to realize some rather grown-up things, such as failure, disappointment, and insecurity. You are finding that everything may not always turn out perfectly, that your parents don't really know everything after all, that pets and people die or go away, and that there aren't easy answers to some of life's big questions.

You are now starting to think a lot more for yourself. That's great, but it means you have more of your own new opinions, ideas, and ways of doing things. The same old way you've done things all your life may not work or "fit" for you anymore. It's exciting, but sometimes hard, to find new ways of living.

Your friends are changing, too, and their feelings are bouncing around just as much as yours are. When you're around each other, you may be getting along one minute and getting on each other's nerves the next.

As you grow up into your own person, you may suddenly start to look at your parents (and grown-ups in general) and think they don't understand you and how you feel. This can be very irritating for both you and your parents. Sometimes you feel like your old self and enjoy being around your family. The next day your mom or dad says or does something that makes you totally furious. Then you're sure you come from a family of real dweebs! Your poor parents are left standing there wondering what on earth they did to upset you, and you are amazed that they don't even know. Clueless!

Remember that your body is changing, too. Inside, your "hormones" are on the move, and you're growing, fast! (Your hormones are the part of you that helps your body grow, develop, and follow the right "schedule." They can also influence how you feel.) You are still in charge of how you choose to act, but be gentle with your body and yourself, knowing you're having new experiences. Like what? Like getting ready for the physical growth and changes you've heard about—height, hair growth, breast development, your menstrual period, weight gain, skin and body odor changes, and even more.

There are a lot more decisions to make now that your life is getting more complicated and busy. You are being invited to a lot more places and have a lot more friends calling—or you wish the invitations and calls would come. You worry about being left out, rejected, ignored, or talked about. You wonder what others think about you. You want to belong.

When you think about it, so much is going on in your life that it's no wonder your feelings are flip-flopping all over the place. It can be really helpful to write in a diary, send letters to a pen pal, or write poems and stories as a way to express your feelings. Keeping track of how you feel can give you clues to who you are, how you feel about a wide variety of things, what makes your feelings change so quickly, and what you can do when your feelings get all mixed up.

❁ Understanding Your Insides

Learning to understand your inside self is a powerful step toward becoming the kind of girl and woman you want to be. It's important to understand your feelings to help you figure out how to make good decisions about your life. Understanding also makes it easier to get your needs and wants met. You can learn to catch your negative, scary emotions and turn them around to something better. Sometimes life is going to be hard. Sometimes bad things really do happen. When they do, you need to know how to cope with your feelings. You will need to know your inside self to help you meet the challenges ahead and come out in one piece.

JOURNALS, DIARIES, & SECRET LETTERS

A journal or a diary is a special place to record all your innermost thoughts, feelings, ideas, and dreams. When you write in a journal, you are telling yourself that you are imporant enough to write about. A special notebook helps you keep track of your writing and is also easier to hide and keep private. You can always share your writing if you wish, but journals and diaries are really meant to be just for you to record your private thoughts and feelings.

You can also write pretend "secret" letters to other people. You can write a "love letter" or get your angry feelings off your chest by pretending to write to the person you're mad at. Maybe you just wish you could tell that other person what's on your mind, but feel too embarrassed or unsure of how to do it. With secret letters you can write to your heart's content without having to send the letters for real. If you have a lot of positive or negative feelings about someone, you can sort them out in a "letter" and then decide how to express some of them to the person directly. Remember, it's important not to keep your thoughts and feelings bottled up inside without ever telling the other person. Letters give you a chance to "get it all out" in private, sort things out, think about it, sleep on it, and then decide what you want to say in real life.

NAME **Those** FEELINGS

Sometimes it's easy to get confused about what's a feeling and what's an idea, or a thought, or some other part of you. First of all, feelings are not things like:

SMART   popular

    sleepy

SICK   HUNGRY

Feelings are things like:

HAPPY   sad   hopeful

silly   **MAD**

grumpy   **calm**

scared   WORRIED

excited   IRRITABLE   GLAD

Feelings are what it's like to be you on the inside. They sometimes seem to change on their own, and yet you do have control over how you express them and even how you feel.

Colorful Feelings

Want to try something fun and artistic? Think about four or five feelings (or as many as you want) that you know you have floating around inside you. Maybe you know that sometime during the week you usually feel happy, frustrated, mad, and excited. Now make a list of your feelings, then give each feeling its own color. For example, happy might have the color yellow, and mad the color red. Any color you choose is just fine. You are in charge!

Feeling . . .	*is like the color . . .*
1. *(example)* Happy	1. Yellow
2.	2.
3.	3.
4.	4.
5.	5.

Now, in the space provided on the next page, draw a design that uses each of the colors of your feelings. Your design doesn't have to be anything "real" looking. It can be swirls and twirls, circles or lines. Any way you choose to draw your feelings is exactly right. Try to use each color as much or as little as you think you usually have that feeling during the week. After you're done, see how much of each color shows up. Are you mostly happy? Sad? Excited? Bored?

When You're in a Seriously **BAD** Mood

Do you ever feel really, really crabby? Sometimes, it seems, for no good reason at all? Maybe someone said something really rude to you, or you didn't get chosen to do something you wanted. Maybe you're just tired and want to be left alone to feel rotten. Well, it happens to all of us. Everybody feels that way sometimes. The trouble is, everybody seems to get mad at you when it's your turn to be a crab! What do you do about it? Here's Megan:

Megan felt crabby, just plain crabby. Nothing was going right—I mean, nothing. Her brain had turned to complete mush during her social studies test and she figured she'd probably failed it, she wondered why she'd chosen such a stupid-looking outfit to wear today, Kristen told her that Andrea was mad at her but she didn't know why, she couldn't believe the gross stuff they had at school for lunch, and her mom yelled at her for something she didn't even do! And if that wasn't bad enough, she started to cry at school, right in front of everyone. She was so embarrassed. Megan had a serious headache and decided she was going to sit in her closet for the rest of her life and never, ever come out again.

What Now?

Actually, Megan has a pretty good idea. It's perfectly okay to find what works for you to help you feel better. Hiding out in your room (rather than your closet) and taking a long nap may be just the right thing to get yourself glued back together.

Don't panic too early. You (or Megan) may have indeed done a lousy job on the test. But wait to see what the real score is before pulling your hair out. And, if the test was a complete disaster, think of at least three things to do differently when studying for the next test. Maybe ask a parent to quiz you, or reread your notes before you go to sleep.

Clean up any problems before they get too big to handle. Megan could go directly to Andrea and check out if there's a problem and what it is. With her mom, she could admit she was having a rotten day and ask for some time alone, but in a pleasant way. If she was totally in the right, perhaps she could explain the facts to her mom (without blowing up).

What to do about lunch and clothes? Bring a snack and keep it in a locker for really bad lunch days and always try to pick out the next day's clothes the night before so there are no last-minute-in-a-rush-grab-whatever disasters.

Ask for what you need. If you're feeling like life's a mess, maybe a hug would help. Ask your parents, your grandparents, or your brother or sister for a hug, and say how crummy you're feeling. Ask the person to tell you at least one nice thing about yourself to remind you how wonderful you really are and that things will be better tomorrow.

Dear Brave New Girl:
I don't want to tell anybody this because they'll laugh at me, but sometimes I feel really, really scared. I get these weird fears that don't go away, no matter what I do. I get scared about things like someone climbing in my window at night and kidnapping me, or something bad happening to my dad when he travels, or that my house will blow up when I'm away at school, or that I have a bad disease. Stuff like that. I know that it's probably not going to happen, and I feel silly even saying it, but I feel worried anyway. What can I do?
      SIGNED,
      MS. WORRYWART

Dear Ms. Worrywart:
First, you are a brave kid for having the guts to talk about your fears and say them out loud.

    That is step one: telling someone your fears so you aren't alone with them. Now, try to find someone in your life you can talk to about your fears. I bet if you tell your parents and let them know you really are afraid of this stuff, they won't laugh. Sharing your fears with someone makes them seem a lot smaller because you're not alone with them. Other people can help you figure out what to do when you feel afraid.

    That's step two: figuring out what to do when you feel scared. Here's some ideas:

❀   Turn on the lights if it's dark.

❀   Talk to yourself out loud. Give yourself comforting messages like, "I know my dad's going to be fine and he said he'd call tomorrow," or, "I'm really very safe. I can always call my parents or my friends and talk to them."

❀   Play some music if you're home alone. The extra sound in the house can be helpful.

❀   Remind yourself how you solved this problem last time and try that again.

❀   Try changing your activity to doing something you really enjoy. Sometimes getting your mind off your worry helps it disappear.

❀ Try to get to the bottom of your worry. Is something else bothering you? Are your parents fighting? Is school too hard? Are your friends mad at you? Sometimes when other big stuff is going on in our lives, we focus on all the little worries rather than deal with the real and very big problem. If there is a big problem in your life, talk to an adult about it. Never sit alone with your problems.

Sometimes your worries make a lot of sense. For instance, if you have a piano recital or a big test coming up, you're going to feel rather nervous. Those butterflies in your stomach are telling you to study, practice, and work hard so you do your best. Other times, though, it's hard to put your finger on just what you're fearful, scared, or worried about. Maybe you have a headache or a stomachache. You might feel tired or tense. It might be helpful to think about a few fears and worries that are pretty common with girls your age. You're not weird at all if you feel these things sometimes. Then we'll talk about what you and your parents can do to help these fears take a hike and leave you alone.

FEAR BUSTERS

Do these fears sound familiar to you?

Fears that something bad will happen to you or your parents—especially things like burglars coming into your house at night, car accidents, sickness, and even fears that someone will die.

Fears that others won't like you or include you in their plans.

Fears that you will look stupid if you do something such as answer questions at school, trip during gym class, get up in front of a group, or do something that makes everyone look at you.

Fears that your body doesn't look right. You may think you look fat, your hair looks dumb, you have the "wrong" clothes on, your voice sounds all wrong, or everyone is secretly looking at you and thinking there's something wrong with the way you look. You think everyone thinks you look like a dork.

Fears that something has happened if your parents are late getting home.

Fear of the dark and/or of being alone.

Fears that really weird and unusual things are going to happen. Things that you know in your head aren't real, but that worry you anyway. Things like your house is going to blow up, there's someone hiding under your bed, or a plane is going to crash into your house.

Fears of bigger things you may have to confront in your daily life, such as riding in elevators, taking airplane trips, swimming in deep water, getting lost in the woods during a camping trip, going on scary rides at an amusement park, climbing rocks, or taking trips away from home.

These are just a few of the common fears girls like you may experience everyday. Now think a minute and write down a few of your own fears. Don't worry—they won't seem strange or weird at all. Most people have a few common, ordinary, "normal" fears and a few really strange fears. Write your biggies as well as your more secret ones:

1.

2.

3.

4.

5.

Taking Charge

So, now what are you supposed to do with the fears that try to eat up all your fun—the ones that make some days less fun than others, the ones that make you just want to stay home and hide instead of going out and having a great time?

IT'S OKAY TO ASK FOR HELP

It really is okay to ask for help. You don't have to be brave all the time and try to fight these fears alone. You may be afraid your parents or friends will laugh at you if you tell them about your fears. Try to work up your courage as best you can and tell your parents that you want to talk to them about something really important to you. Tell them that it's important that they listen carefully. It's your parents job to help you solve your problems with fears. You don't have to feel like you're expecting too much if you ask them for their help. That's what parents are for! (You can tell them I said so.)

You're Not Being Silly

The rest of the world sometimes still thinks girls' and women's feelings are silly or ridiculous. People might roll their eyes and act like they think girls are too emotional. You don't need to feel ashamed or embarrassed about expressing your feelings. You don't always have to remain calm, and you certainly don't always have to be sweet and nice. It's normal not to feel happy or perky all the time.

Getting Some Control in My Life

It can be helpful to find specific areas in your life where you really can have some control. This way you can direct some of your energy into these areas so that you feel confident and powerful. Talk to your parents about finding places in your life where you can be totally in charge, areas such as:

how you keep your room (although many parents want you to keep it somewhat picked up)

how you wear your hair

how you handle your allowance money

how you spend Saturday mornings

 HOW YOU CHOOSE TO DO ANYTHING
SPECIAL YOU AND YOUR PARENTS AGREE ON

It feels good to be able to do some things just the way you want to and need to with no one else controlling you.

Bravery: Proving to Yourself That You Can Do It

It's important to prove to yourself that you can handle your fears and problems. Being brave can be tough, especially when you're feeling seriously scared. And besides, wimping out is not such a bad thing to do sometimes. Eventually, though, it's a good idea to figure out how to fight back against your fears and problems and solve them once and for all.

Goals for Getting Rid of Fears & Worries

Although fears and worries are not funny, and they're hard work to get rid of, let's think of them for a moment as nasty bugs that buzz around your head and generally drive you crazy. To fight back you need some good old-fashioned bug spray. Let's take a moment to develop your own "bug spray" to ward off the bugs of fear.

Go back for a minute to your fears list you made a few
pages back. Now take each fear that you listed and write
down at least two things you can do to fight that fear.
Now ask your parent(s) to help you think of two more creative ways you can squish the fear.

Fear	What I can do to squish my fear
1.	1.
	2.
	3.
	4.
2.	1.
	2.
	3.
	4.
3.	1.
	2.
	3.
	4.
4.	1.
	2.
	3.
	4.

Congratulations! You are on your way to overcoming your
fears and worries. Now you need help to follow through
on these ideas and practice them until you feel confident
that your solutions will work.

Do I Always Have to be Brave?

No! You don't always have to be brave. It's okay to cry, be scared, shake like a leaf, and feel like throwing up. Let's take a quiz about when you feel afraid and worried and when you feel great and confident. On a scale of 1 to 10 (with 1 = very little and 10 = a lot), answer these questions about yourself, then add your numbers to find your score:

1. I feel scared or nervous:

1   2   3   4   5   6   7   8   9   10

2. I feel like a nervous wreck or in a total panic:

1   2   3   4   5   6   7   8   9   10

3. I feel like I can handle most of my problems:

1   2   3   4   5   6   7   8   9   10

4. I think most of my feelings are pretty normal:

1   2   3   4   5   6   7   8   9   10

5. I have a few people (like parents/friends/teachers) who I know will help me handle any problem that I have:

1   2   3   4   5   6   7   8   9   10

Name three people who can help you solve problems:

6. I feel the most scared when:

7. I feel brave and confident when:

8. I usually come up with good ideas about how to solve my problems:

1   2   3   4   5   6   7   8   9   10

YOUR SCORE

0–28: You're beginning to learn how to handle your fears and worries. You're understanding that it's okay to ask for help and tell others how you feel so you're not alone with your problems. Keep up the good work, and you'll feel less fearful and a lot happier.

29–35: You're beginning to develop courage and find solutions to your problems. You realize everyone gets scared and nervous sometimes and you find ways to turn things around so you feel better.

36+: You're on your way to solving your problems and feeling good about yourself and life. You ask for help when you need it and have worked hard to come up with creative ideas to help you get "unstuck" when facing a challenge. Go, girl!

I Wonder if I'm Normal?

Sophie is twelve years old. She plays a mean game of soccer, aces her math quizzes, and zooms around the Internet on the computer. She lives in jeans, sweatshirts, and weird tennis shoes. She thinks her English teacher is way too odd and her parents are totally mean for making her go to bed by 9:30 on school nights. Her little sister drives her crazy one minute and they play great private games together the next. She's got a ton of friends who call all the time and she thinks the school lunches are made by cooks from another planet. She usually has lots of energy, but sometimes crashes after a busy week and worries like crazy about her grades. She loves to play the violin, but hates to practice. She likes how she looks but wishes her voice sounded different. She gets stomachaches when she worries; one day she's not really all that hungry and the next she could eat the entire refrigerator, door included.

Think about Sophie for a minute. All in all, Sophie sounds totally normal, wouldn't you say? And yet, Sophie wonders if she's like everybody else. She thinks other people know how to do everything better and wonders if they know some sort of secret. She wishes she could look as cool and calm as other people she sees.

Actually, Sophie is doing a great job of living. She needs to learn to be nicer to herself and not be so hard on herself. Some people really push themselves to try to be perfect. Do you find yourself doing that? Being normal simply means being yourself and liking who you are. There are going to be things you do or think that are different from others, and that's wonderfully okay. If everyone looked and acted exactly the same, the world would be really boring!

Being Different

Being different is tough for many growing girls. Lots of girls want to be just like their friends. They call each other up on the phone after school to check out how their friends did on the French test, what they thought of morning assembly, or what they're going to wear to the Friday evening dance at school. Checking things out with your friends is a great idea. You learn about them and yourself that way. I'd like to challenge you, though, to also let the real you out. Let the world see who you are.

Hurt Feelings

Catherine couldn't believe her ears. Her very best friend Caroline had just told her that Erica was having a huge sleepover and Catherine wasn't invited. It's true that Catherine and Erica weren't all-time best friends or anything, but still, they all hung out together and sat together at lunch. Catherine was hurt but didn't want to show it, so she just acted like she didn't care one bit. But in fact, she did care, and her feelings were very, very hurt. Should Catherine:

a.   Tell Erica she hated her and never wanted to speak to her again?

b.   Spread a nasty rumor about Erica that wasn't true, but would hurt her feelings like Catherine's were hurt?

c.   Remain friendly with Erica, saying "hello" and being fairly pleasant?

d.   Talk to Erica and ask her why she wasn't invited?

e.   Ask Caroline to ask Erica why Catherine wasn't invited?

f.   Completely ignore Erica and act like she doesn't live on this planet?

WHAT WOULD YOU DO?

*Can you think of a better, more creative
way to handle this situation?*

Hurt feelings can be pretty painful. You want to disappear into the woodwork. When your feelings have been hurt, you may also feel really embarrassed and wish you could move to Mars and start a new life all over where no one knows you. It's hard to talk about hurt feelings because you're afraid you're going to cry or say something dumb. It's important to get hurt feelings out into the open, though, so they don't just sit there inside you causing nasty thoughts and feelings to grow. Sometimes when girls feel hurt, it turns into anger or sadness. Then instead of being clear and direct about what's really going on inside, some girls have a freak-attack or sit in their rooms, crying and feeling awful.

WHAT CAN I DO IF MY FEELINGS ARE HURT?

Here are some ideas of actions you can take if your feelings get squashed.

Talk to someone about how bad you feel. Tell a parent or friend what happened and how it's making you feel. Don't keep those sad feelings to yourself.

Think of one or two things you could say to the people who hurt you to let them know how what they did made you feel. Sometimes people don't even realize that something they did hurt you. They need to know.

Write your feelings in a diary or secret letter to help get them outside you and on a piece of paper instead.

Let yourself release all your feelings. Cry, feel mad, hurt, surprised, or whatever else comes up.

Think about whether this person is "safe" to be in a relationship with. Has he or she hurt your feelings many times before? Do you end up hurt and angry almost every time you're together? This is a "red flag" that may be telling you this person isn't a healthy, happy friend for you to be around. You may need to find a new friend. You deserve to be treated well and not hurt all the time!

ANGER: HOT & HEAVY Feelings

You know the days. First, your mom yells at you because you're late getting up and she makes it sound like the school bus is going to leave you behind. Then, your sister crabs at you for getting in her way in the bathroom (you were just trying to brush your teeth!). Then you get to school and realize you left your math assignment on the kitchen table and your teacher glares at you when you tell him. Your friend Angel acts like a snot and you have no idea what you did wrong. Now she won't sit with you at lunch. After school you're in trouble again for not cleaning the hamster cage and your dad tells you to turn off the TV until you get your chores done. And dinner? Whoever invented that weird stuff your dad made should be pushed off the planet. The fun continues after dinner with a ton of homework all in one night. You wonder why you bothered to get up this morning. What a disgusting day it's been.

What Kinds of Things Bug You?

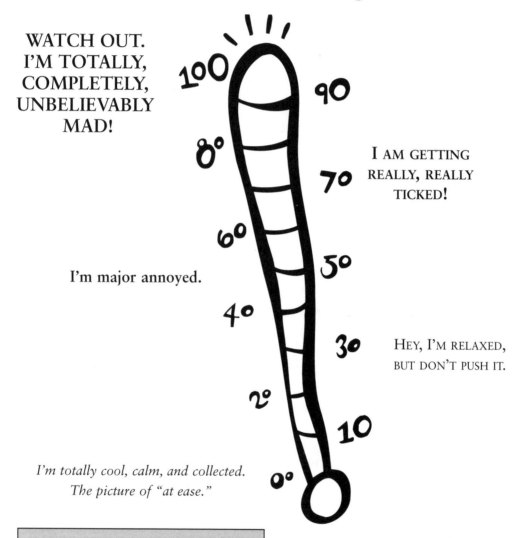

WATCH OUT.
I'M TOTALLY,
COMPLETELY,
UNBELIEVABLY
MAD!

100 90

8°

70 I AM GETTING
REALLY, REALLY
TICKED!

60 50

I'm major annoyed.

4°

30 HEY, I'M RELAXED,
BUT DON'T PUSH IT.

2°

10

I'm totally cool, calm, and collected.
The picture of "at ease."

0°

You're certainly not responsible for every crummy thing that happens to you. But you are totally and completely responsible and in charge of how you respond to bad things that happen.

How "hot" does your temper get with the situations listed below? Rate yourself using the thermometer on this page. Decide how mad each of the following situations would make you and put the "temperature" number in the space.

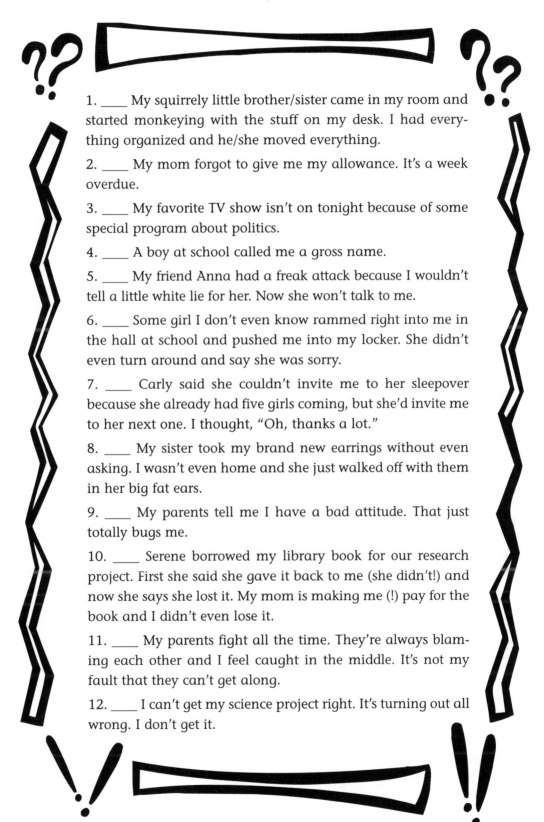

1. ____ My squirrely little brother/sister came in my room and started monkeying with the stuff on my desk. I had everything organized and he/she moved everything.

2. ____ My mom forgot to give me my allowance. It's a week overdue.

3. ____ My favorite TV show isn't on tonight because of some special program about politics.

4. ____ A boy at school called me a gross name.

5. ____ My friend Anna had a freak attack because I wouldn't tell a little white lie for her. Now she won't talk to me.

6. ____ Some girl I don't even know rammed right into me in the hall at school and pushed me into my locker. She didn't even turn around and say she was sorry.

7. ____ Carly said she couldn't invite me to her sleepover because she already had five girls coming, but she'd invite me to her next one. I thought, "Oh, thanks a lot."

8. ____ My sister took my brand new earrings without even asking. I wasn't even home and she just walked off with them in her big fat ears.

9. ____ My parents tell me I have a bad attitude. That just totally bugs me.

10. ____ Serene borrowed my library book for our research project. First she said she gave it back to me (she didn't!) and now she says she lost it. My mom is making me (!) pay for the book and I didn't even lose it.

11. ____ My parents fight all the time. They're always blaming each other and I feel caught in the middle. It's not my fault that they can't get along.

12. ____ I can't get my science project right. It's turning out all wrong. I don't get it.

How to CHILL OUT
When You're **MAD, MAD, MAD**

Step One: Know what it is that makes you mad. Write about it. Make a list.

Step Two: Take a minute (or ten or twenty) to get a grip, calm down, and feel like you have some control over your feelings. If you react too quickly, you'll start yelling and stomping off and saying things that get you into an even worse mess.

Step Three: Decide on a scale of 1 to 10 how bad of a problem it is or how angry you are. This will help you decide how to handle what's happening. Is it a minor nuisance, like a mosquito, or a huge disaster, like you're failing social studies?

Step Four: Try to speak calmly, but clearly and firmly, about your feelings. Always start your sentences with "I," such as "I feel really angry about what you just did." If you start pointing your finger and blaming the other person, they'll get worked up and the fight will just continue. Remember: "I think, I feel, I want . . . " not "Why don't you . . . . "

Step Five: Decide what you can fix or control and what is going to happen no matter what you do. You can't and don't have to solve every problem, so let go of the parts you can't change. Then decide what actions you can take to make things better.

Ideas for Actions I Can Take to Feel Less Angry

❀ Talk to the person who may have caused the situation. Tell her or him how you feel, making "I" statements.

❀ Do something you like to do for a while until you can calm down and think clearly.

❀ Get suggestions or advice from someone who has been through what you're feeling.

❀ Get some exercise to help get rid of that angry, nervous feeling. Go for a walk, run, or ride your bike.

❀ Try to think ahead about what kinds of people and situations make you really mad. Decide if it's a good idea to be around them, or if it's best to stay away from the situation for a while.

Write your own idea or two about what works for you:

Fruit Basket Upset

Sometimes every feeling you've ever known comes flying to the surface, especially if something really big is happening in your life. You don't know which feeling to tackle first, there are so many. Think about Ginny for a moment:

Ginny's parents were getting divorced. "It's probably better this way," she thought. "All they do is fight and yell. I can't stand it anymore." Still, she felt scared and worried about how life was going to be. She was afraid that she'd hardly ever get a chance to see her dad, and now her mom had to work a lot more than she did before all this happened. Ginny would come home alone after school and let herself in, and stay by herself until her mother got home at 5:30. She was so sad, but mad, too. She wondered, "Why can't these people get along? After all, they're grown-ups and should be able to figure things out!" She felt mad because she felt like she was losing her family because these two grown-ups couldn't act like normal people. So, there she sat, mad, sad, worried, and lonely. "Doesn't anyone care about what I feel and what I think?" thought Ginny.

Some Ideas for Ginny

Remember that her parents love her, even if they don't get along with each other.

Ginny doesn't have to sit and listen to her dad put her mom down, or her mom say nasty things about her dad. She can tell them, "I don't want to hear bad things about my other parent. I love you both." She should stay away from two fighting adults.

Always remember that it's not her fault that her parents are getting divorced.

Don't try to make grown-up decisions. Let her parents worry about their own problems.

Tell each parent how she feels right away, rather than letting the feelings get overwhelming.

HERE'S SANDY

Things at home were such a mess that Sandy and her brother had gone to live with another family (a "foster family") until her own family could solve some of their problems. Sometimes Sandy just loved being with her new, "temporary" family. They seemed so together. Gayle, the mother, always had dinner ready and Sam, the dad, always seemed to have time to help Sandy with her homework or to shoot baskets.

There was always time to talk and nobody yelled at her. In fact, everyone seemed to enjoy each other and people laughed a lot at the dinner table. At her own house, everyone was always coming and going, fighting, or working. And when her dad drank, everything was a total disaster. She usually ended up making herself a cheese sandwich for supper and was always behind in her homework. No one seemed to care when or where she went or what time she got to bed, and yet, Sandy loved her mom and dad, and she missed her own room. Talk about mixed-up feelings.

Use your smarts and think up three things that are important for Sandy to do every day:

1.

2.

3.

Grow Your Own

HAPPINESS

It seems like some people never smile. You almost want to go up to them and whisper, "Hey, you know it's okay to smile and be happy sometimes." Then there are other people who seem to have a goofy, huge smile on their faces all the time. It's like someone plugged them into an electrical outlet. These people are almost too happy.

How about you?
Where do you fall on the Happiness Scale?

HAPPINESS SCALE

1. I giggle and laugh a lot.

        True   False

2. I wake up in the morning pretty cheerful.

        True   False

3. I'm in a good mood most of the time.

        True   False

4. I love life and have a great time nearly every day.

        True   False

5. Lots of people like me and say I'm fun to be around.

        True   False

6. I think I have a good attitude most of the time.

        True   False

7. Grumpy? Who me? Not very often!

        True   False

8. It takes a lot before I really get mad.

        True   False

9. I'm pretty easy-going. Not much gets on my nerves.

        True   False

10. I like life. Life likes me.

        True   False

YOUR SCORE

9–10 TRUES: You are indeed a rather cheery sort of girl. Not much gets you down and if you get crabby and grumpy, you bounce back almost right away.

7–8 TRUES: You have your ups and downs, but for the most part you feel good about your life.

6 or fewer TRUES: Maybe you're a more serious girl, or perhaps you have some troubles that worry you and leave you feeling a bit less happy than you would like. It might be helpful to talk to someone when you're feeling down or worried and get some help to find your way back to a happier place.

Things I Can Do Today to Help Myself Feel Happy

You can't always keep nasty things from happening to you in this world. Sometimes bad stuff happens to you and it really is your own fault. You might get a lousy grade in English because you didn't bother to hand in your book report (truth be told, you didn't even get around to reading the book). But, other times bad things happen just because they sometimes do in life.

When bad things happen, you decide how you will react. In other words, you can choose how you want to feel about yourself and your life. It may take a while to work through difficult feelings (like sadness, anger, and loneliness), but you can do it. You don't have to stay miserable.

Think of five things you could do today that you know would help you feel better about yourself and life. Happiness comes from the inside, but it sometimes comes faster if we're doing things we enjoy or are around people who make us feel happy and interested in life.

Feel Good by Helping Others Feel Better

Meredith was feeling kind of bored. She was hanging out in her backyard wondering what to do with her wide-open afternoon when she spotted Mrs. Burke down the block trying to bag her leaves and weeds. She smiled as she remembered that Mrs. Burke always used to give her and her friends chocolate chip cookies, fresh and warm out of the oven, when she was just a little kid. Suddenly Meredith knew exactly what to do with her afternoon. Mrs. Burke smiled and thanked Meredith over and over for all her help with the yard work—and would you believe she had just baked some cookies that morning? Meredith totally pigged out and ate six of them before heading home.

Meredith found the perfect solution to her own feelings of boredom. What a great way to feel better about the day, and Mrs. Burke wouldn't have a sore back tomorrow, either.

Chapter 3

Friends FOREVER

The Social You

Are you a social butterfly? A quiet bookworm? A noisy, active sports fan? Answer these questions for a glimpse at your social personality:

1. I love to be around lots of people.

        Yes   **No**

2. I prefer to quietly curl up on my bed and read than be around others.

        Yes   **No**

3. Put me in the middle of the action!

        Yes   **No**

4. I just love to be the center of attention.

        Yes   **No**

5. I'd rather kiss my brother than get up on stage and talk into a microphone.

        Yes   **No**

6. Let me run like the wind in a good, fast, outdoor game.

        Yes   **No**

7. I'd rather play a calm board game or cards.

        Yes   **No**

8. I have a ton of friends who call me and want to do stuff on the weekend.

         Yes   **No**

9. I'm more comfortable with one or two really close friends who know me well.

         Yes   **No**

10. I like big, noisy birthday parties or sleepovers.

         Yes   **No**

Study your answers for a minute. Do you see a pattern? Do you seem to prefer action, or a quieter approach to the social scene? It doesn't matter if you are an in-your-face-let-me-at-'em kind of girl or the shy, quiet, sensitive type. What's important is to accept yourself for who you are and develop the kind of friendships that are best for you.

Friends are the Best!

I always hang out with:

My all time best friend(s) is/are:

We are alike because:

I am different from my friend(s), though, because:

Here's Molly

Molly's family had moved over the summer and she would be starting a new school this year. Just thinking about it made Molly's stomach drop like a roller coaster. What if no one liked her or talked to her? How embarrassing. "I'll just die," she thought, "if I have to eat lunch alone in that huge lunchroom. I know I had plenty of friends at my old school, but what if everyone just ignores me here? I've heard some schools are really snotty." Molly's parents tried to convince her that everything would be just fine, but Molly didn't exactly believe them. What could Molly do to feel accepted?

Molly is scared, of course. Who wouldn't be? But a warm, friendly smile will go a long way toward giving other kids the message that she is someone they will want to know and be friends with.

Molly can work on having a positive outlook and act like she's interested in being friends.

SHE COULD TALK OVER HER FEARS WITH HER PARENTS AND ASK THEM TO HELP HER FIGURE OUT WHAT TO DO.

Use the "rule of inclusion," which means everyone is included in games, lunchtime, and activities. No one is left out—it's not allowed. Some schools already have this rule in place and it helps everyone, active or quiet, old or new, feel like they belong, and you know what a good feeling that is!

What could the girls at her new school do to help Molly feel welcome?

The teacher could assign Molly "buddies" to be her "friends for the day." These could be different buddies, such as one to have lunch with her, one to hang out during flex-time with her, another to make sure she gets to classes, the bathroom, the gym, etc. You get the picture. Molly shouldn't have to be left alone at all during her first week at school.

Remember these tips when someone is new at your school. If your school doesn't have these two rules, why not bring them up with your teacher or student council representative?

Girls at school could call Molly and invite her to join them for an upcoming event, or offer to help her with her homework assignments.

The girls at school could have an open, friendly attitude that says "welcome" to Molly. Being stand-offish or giving her the cold shoulder would be a mean and hurtful thing to do. Nobody wants to be treated like that. Keep in mind that someday that "new girl" could be you!

UP & *Down* FRIENDSHIPS

Do you sometimes have friendships that seem to bounce all over the place? One day everything is going great, and the next day, everything's a mess. You may have noticed that you hardly ever seem to fight at all with some of your friends, while with others, it's more like a roller coaster. Personalities can sure get in the way, even when you're trying to be good friends.

Dear Brave New Girl:
Sometimes my best friend just ignores me. We get along great and then someone else asks her to do something and they go off and leave me behind. I feel really stupid just standing there, knowing I'm not invited. They don't seem to care about me. What should I do when this happens?
> Signed,
> Left Out

Dear Left Out:
It's really hard when your best friend acts like you don't exist. You expect her to care about you and your feelings. Your feelings are hurt and you tend to think, "I'd never do that to her!" Unfortunately, we all treat others less than perfectly sometimes. It's important to remember how lousy you feel when others do this to you and remind yourself to try never to do this to someone else. Here's some ideas for handling your hurt feelings and fixing a messy relationship situation:

Don't gossip and say bad things about what happened with your friend. Talking about her behind her back is just going to make things worse.

Do seek out your other friends for company and fun.

When you feel a little better (say, in a day or two), consider telling your best friend how you felt—hurt, surprised, and left out. She might not have even realized that she hurt your feelings or made you mad. She probably didn't mean to.

Always keep your circle of friends growing and expanding. It's good to not rely on only one person to be your friend all the time. The more friends you have, the better chance you'll have of having a fun time planned and someone you like to share it with.

Here's Ashley and Erica

Ashley and Erica were the best of friends. They could hardly wait to go to Ashley's family cabin for the weekend. They got along great at school and thought a weekend together would be fabulous. Well, guess what? About halfway through the weekend, Erica felt like Ashley had turned into a bossy cow and Ashley began to think Erica was a real bore.

Here's Kelly and Becca

Kelly and Becca immediately raised their hands to work on a major project at school together. They always got along great and could hardly be separated during the school day. Kelly and Becca divided up the project tasks and planned to get together for a sleepover at Kelly's house on Friday to put their project together. By Friday, Kelly had gathered all her information and had everything lined up on her desk ready for the sleepover. Becca showed up completely unprepared, with a million excuses and promises to get it done by next week. Kelly was really mad at Becca and wondered when they would possibly have time to get everything together.

What happened to Ashley and Erica, Kelly and Becca? When these girls got together outside of school, they each saw a "different side" of their friend.

Ashley wasn't expecting Erica to want to sleep until noon, and Erica wasn't planning on Ashley wanting to get up at the crack of dawn and go-go-go all day. Kelly was always super-organized about her schoolwork and had no idea that Becca was a last-minute type of girl. Becca couldn't understand why Kelly was so freaked-out about finishing the project at a later day.

These girls learned a few lessons in getting to know your friends better. So does this mean these girls can't be friends anymore? Absolutely not. But, next time, it might be wise to plan ahead about schedules, ideas, and "ground rules"!

FAIR AND SQUARE

Isn't it the pits when people act like they know everything about everything? They get bossy and act like Little Miss Know-It-All. Face it, girls, sometimes we all get a little carried away with ourselves and our own sense of importance, thinking we're right and everyone else is wrong. But then it's so embarrassing when we find out we're completely wrong. We wish the floor would just open up and we could disappear. We feel pretty dumb, and yet besides wearing a brown paper bag over our head for a few days or hiding under the covers until the mess blows over, there's not much we can do after we make fools out of ourselves. Don't worry too much, everyone does it sometimes (it just feels totally awful when it's your turn).

Rather than trying to be right all the time, take the time to listen to what the other person is saying. She or he probably has a good point, too.

Remember that everyone sees the world differently. In a way, it's as though everyone has her or his own special "glasses." Interestingly, no one sees the world exactly the way you do, and no one feels or thinks exactly like you, either. It's really rather wonderful.

On one hand, no one else has your special and unique view of the world. On the other hand, you have to allow everyone else to have their thoughts, feelings, and viewpoint as well. It can get complicated trying to figure out when to go along with someone else's viewpoint and when to stand firm with your own.

More Helpful Ideas to Keep You Out of the Pickle Jar with Your Friends

1. Listen carefully to what your friends are saying.

2. Voice your own opinion, clearly and with confidence.

3. Keep in mind that everyone else is going to see the world in a different way and their opinions are just as important and "real" as your own.

4. Use "I" statements when you voice your ideas and opinions. Don't blame others for their "faults." Instead, say things like "I think," "I want," and "I would like."

5. Work hard to come to a compromise. Everyone ends up feeling respected, listened to, and reasonably happy.

6. It's okay to agree to disagree. You and your friends don't always have to agree on everything to be great friends and have tons of fun.

7. Remember, no one person is in charge of the world. Everyone's opinion matters.

In short, having your own opinion is great! Using your voice, talents, and energy to express your opinion is the best way to go. Considering other people's opinions does not mean your opinion has to get lost or fizzle out. You can make sure your opinion is strong, clear, and taken seriously without running over everyone else like a freight train. Never be afraid to say what you think. Bring up your ideas and opinions whenever you get a chance. Each time you do this, you will feel stronger and braver—and next time will be easier.

Rosemary's Top Ten Tips on Making and Keeping Friends

1. Be nice and include everyone. People will get the impression that you are sweet and want to become better friends.

2. Once you've made a friend, don't be like static cling—let the person do other things without you. Your friend can have other friends.

3. Comparing is the pits. Don't always say how you're ugly but your friend is pretty, or you are stupid and your friend is smart. Friends don't know how to respond to that, and most likely you have good qualities, too.

4.   Don't always worry about the really popular kids. What most people want is a nice, trustworthy friend.

5.   Why not give someone a call? If you really want to be a friend, call some-one up and just find something you have in common. Don't call twenty-four hours a day, seven days a week, though; that's a little too friendly.

6.   Let your friends know when you're sad. Good friends know when you are upset, so don't lie and say everything is fine. Nothing is fine all the time, so let it out!

7.   Cute is cute, but dumb isn't. Don't act like you don't know anything because most likely you do know a thing or two. People don't like to explain every detail when they know you know what's going on.

8.   Be yourself! Don't try to be someone you are not. The truth is, you can't be someone you are not, because obviously you are you! Keep your own personality with you and let it shine.

9.   Pretty isn't better. Not everyone is Cindy Crawford or Nikki Taylor, but you may have a great personality. You are you and that is that. So just be your personality, not your looks.

10.   You can never have too many friends. No matter who they are or what they look like, everyone is definitely willing to have a new friend. So be that new friend.

Rosemary Park Shultz, age thirteen, is an eighth grader. Her favorite thing to do is to go places or just be with her friends. She is the proud owner of two chubby goldfish. Her best subjects at school are math and French, and she's a great swimmer.

JEALOUSY

Are you ever bugged out of your brains by someone else because of what she has, how she looks, or what she's able to do that you can't? Jealousy and envy can rear their ugly little heads pretty fast, can't they?

What's **Right** with This Picture?

Do you remember looking at pictures in magazines or restaurant placemats with instructions to find the items that didn't fit in the picture? You know, things like the rabbit eating a hamburger, the bird with two sets of wings, the cow with reindeer antlers. In other words, you were told to look hard and find what's wrong with the picture. That was kind of fun to do, but it taught you to be negative, critical, rejecting, and to find a way to get rid of things that looked "different."

Wouldn't you really rather focus on the positive? Look at the difference between negative, rotten attitudes and a more positive, healthy outlook. Where do you see yourself?

Remember that everyone has problems and bad days. There is nothing wrong with you for having your share. But you, and only you, can decide what kind of general attitude you want to have.

You can be feeling great about your day and then you hear that Erica is taking skiing lessons, Allie has just been chosen to be the lead in the school play, Ellie came to school today wearing the best outfit ever, and Jordana gets to take horseback riding lessons. So much for your "boring" life. What a day! You wish you could have some of what others have so much that you can almost taste it. And you have this incredible urge to say something mean or nasty behind their backs because you're feeling . . . **JEALOUS!**

It's really hard when others seem to have so much, or at least they seem to have something you don't and wish you did. (Of course, you may not have even realized you wanted something until you saw somebody else with it.) You feel like you'd be happier if you could have it, too. Maybe those things would make you happy for a while. But why gossip about it? You know in your heart of hearts that if you say nasty things about a girlfriend because she has or gets something you can't have, it's only going to end up biting you right back. So even if it's hard to smile and think positive, here's some clues to help you stay on track.

Grab a piece of paper and a pencil and make a list of at least ten things you're really grateful for right now in your own life. This helps you refocus on the good stuff happening in your own life when you're down in the dumps.

Think about whether you want to save up some of your own money to purchase the thing you want. (Also be sure to read Chapter 8 for great ideas about how to get some extra cash for the stuff you want.)

Stretch your brain and think of something positive and cheerful to say to the person who just got that certain something you too would like. Compliment her on her cool new outfit or ask to see pictures of her vacation. Show genuine interest—it proves you are a very generous, friendly girl!

Negative Talkers

We all know people who seem grumpy and kind of crabby a lot of the time. Do you ever get tired of listening to your friends, parents, or brothers and sisters complain about everything? Sometimes it seems like nothing is going right. Everybody's griping about something. It's true that sometimes everyone is worried or afraid. Sometimes people really do have something yucky to complain about. And it really helps to tell someone about a problem, get it off your chest, and get some good, solid help about it. Sometimes people just gripe for no real reason. It's a really bad habit.

You know the types of complainers and little dark clouds. One of them is the gossip. This kind of girl always has something negative to say about others. She talks behind people's backs, "backstabs," and gossips. She picks apart everything that other people do and tries to get her friends to agree with her and reject the other person. She may act really nice to someone's face, but say nasty things later behind her back. She gossips about anyone who isn't there at the moment—on the bus, at the lunchroom table . . . .

Then there is the everything-is-wrong girl. This girl complains about life in general. Nothing suits her fancy. She's bored, tired, or thinks everything is stupid. She's a real drag to be around.

Don't forget the "I'm so bad at/I'm so fat/I'm so ugly" girl. This girl tears herself down. She is forever saying crummy things about herself, hoping that you'll disagree and tell her how wonderful she is. This gets pretty boring and frustrating after a while. You wish she'd cut it out.

It's no fun to be around girls like these. Decide right now, once and for all, that you aren't going to be like that. Decide to be positive. The world will love you for it. To quote the name of an old song, decide to "walk on the sunny side of the street."

Sunny Attitudes

It's easy to get seriously crabby sometimes. You feel tired or stressed out, and things aren't going well at school, home, or with your friends. Your little brother is acting like a total nerd and is driving you nuts. Your little sister is acting like she's two years old instead of seven. You wish you lived on another planet. So who feels like being cheerful? It's easy to compare yourself to others, wishing you were somehow different and more like them. You wish you had what they have—more money, nicer clothes, fabulous vacations, a neat bedroom. But, what can you do to cheer yourself up and get back to enjoying life?

Decide to be happy. Yes, that's right. DECIDE. A lot of being happy is a decision. You can decide to look at the gloom and doom, or decide to roll up your sleeves and get to work on a problem so you can be happier.

Walk away from people or situations that constantly drag you down. You don't have to put up with negativity all the time.

If you're worried or frustrated, scared or upset, ask someone older and wiser for help. An adult can help you break your problem into bite-sized solutions so you can handle them and move on to a better place. You don't have to carry your problems around by yourself.

Practice treating other girls the way you would like to be treated yourself.

When Friends Head off in the **WRONG** Direction

Jillian didn't know if she should blab or not. She heard from Betsy that Andrea had shoplifted her "new" sweater when she went to the mall last Saturday.

Suzy was really worried because her friend Ellen was so upset she said she would kill herself.

Kiki was a mess because she knew that Joni took the money from Nancy's locker.

Boni was a nervous wreck because her friend Alicia was making plans to run away from home this weekend.

What do you do when you know your friend is heading in a great big hurry down the wrong road—a road that will get her in major trouble and cause her endless problems? You can't exactly demand that she take your advice, and you can't expect someone to live her life the way you think she should (even if you know you are right). Your friends' lives are their own—they're in charge of themselves. So what is a friend to do? Watch a great girl jump into disaster?

IT'S PERFECTLY OKAY TO TELL

It's not only perfectly okay to tell an adult when you're really worried about your friend, you may be helping her more than you can ever imagine. She may be too scared, worried, or confused to know what to do to help herself. Grown-ups certainly aren't perfect, but they have good ideas and more power to help solve big problems. In fact, if you don't tell, your friend may never get the help she needs to feel better. What kinds of things are worth telling an adult about? Here are a few ideas:

If your friend tells you someone is abusing her. This is a must-tell situation.

If your friend says she's going to hurt (or kill) herself or someone else, you must, must, must tell. Take this seriously, even if you think she's just kidding. She may actually be thinking about it or have such a huge problem that she doesn't know what else to do.

If you find out your friend is seriously cheating on schoolwork or lying through her teeth, saying she didn't do something that she really did (and it's serious).

If you think your friend might run away.

If your friend is in a dangerous relationship with a boy.

If your friend is stealing stuff. Anything. It's not okay.

Here are some ideas of what to do and not do:

DO	DON'T
1. Tell her you're concerned and worried.	1. Nag, nag, nag.
2. Tell an adult if it's really serious.	2. Keep a serious mess to yourself.
3. Be a good friend.	3. Go along with her and get into a big fat mess of trouble yourself.

DO	DON'T
4. Offer her another good idea you might have that would keep her out of trouble.	4. Think her ideas are the only ones.
5. Think for yourself! What's right for you?	5. Accept her view of the situation.
6. Keep your own nose clean.	6. Get caught up in bad decisions.
7. Offer to go along with your friend to talk this over with an adult you trust.	7. Keep bad stuff a secret.
8. Tell her you can't be friends for now, if what she's doing is wrong.	8. Stay friends if it means bad news and big problems for you.

You get the picture. If you think your friend is doing something that could really hurt her or get her in major trouble, it's time to break the silence and get help!

BOYS

So do you talk with them, hang out with them, play ball with them, talk on the phone with them, kiss them? I mean, what exactly are you supposed to do with these weird creatures called boys?

Discovering boys and considering the possibility of kissing one of them is a huge step for a girl. Suddenly, these total dweebs are starting to look a little bit interesting. Then one of them calls you on the phone or sits with you at lunch. He wants to "go together." Do you actually kiss him? Some of you are thinking, "Gross!" "Yuck," "Disgusting, totally, disgusting," and some of you are thinking, "Wellllll . . . maaaaybe . . . how do I know when?" Or, rather, "How do I know how?" (You can relax—there is no one right way to kiss.) Now what?

Healthy Boy-Girl Relationships

Healthy	The Pits
1. You both get to do some of what you like to do.	1. You always end up doing what he wants to do.
2. He is respectful in the way he talks and treats you.	2. He acts like he owns you.
3. You enjoy being with him.	3. You only stay with him because there doesn't seem to be anyone else.
4. He keeps his paws to himself.	4. He tries to touch you in ways that make you uncomfortable.
5. Your friends like him.	5. Your friends think you're nuts to hang out with a creep like him.
6. He listens to what you say.	6. He does all the talking and expects you to act interested only in him.
7. He shows he cares about your feelings, too.	7. He obviously doesn't care what you feel.
8. He's willing to meet and be polite to your family.	8. He doesn't want to come around or meet your family.
9. He likes you just the way you are.	9. He's always trying to change something about you.
10. He's got a good future ahead of him.	10. He's headed toward being a real loser.

NEWS FLASH!

You're used to kissing (or getting kissed by) your granny, your parents, and dear old Great Aunt Ethel. Kissing a boy is something altogether different.

Your first few relationships will be short and hopefully sweet. You probably won't meet and marry your soulmate at age twelve. Remember, you have lots of time to practice and get this boy-girl thing right.

No boy is worth giving up who you really are. Don't stop doing the things you like to do just because he might not want to do them.

Don't worry about being "dumped." If you aren't right for each other, you'll just naturally drift apart. Or, if you don't like him, you don't have to stick around and wait to be hurt.

Remember, boys are just people—nothing more, nothing less.

Here are some mini-stories of healthy boy/girl relationships and some red flags that tell you a boy is getting way too serious or out-of-line. Take a look at a couple of these examples and decide what you think.

Jamie saw David coming down the hall at school and wasn't sure if she was nervous or scared. David always wanted to corner her at lunch or on the hallway corners. He seemed nice enough, but he was always showing up or following her wherever she went. She really didn't like it and wanted to tell him to stop.

Amber was thrilled that Eric called her after school on Friday. He just wanted to talk about stuff that had happened at school and what she got on the math test. They talked for a few minutes and he asked her if she wanted to eat lunch with him on Monday. Amber said, "Sure." After they hung up, she called absolutely everyone she knew to tell them that Eric had actually called her and wanted to sit with her.

Ashley was sick and tired of Ben calling her all the time. She had other things to do and he was always asking her what she was going to do. She almost felt like he thought he owned her and she needed to ask permission. Yuck!

Becca felt all goosepimply when Justin lightly put his arm around her at the seventh grade dance. She'd never felt like this before!

How do you know when it's good and when it's yucky? Notice how each girl felt around the boy. You can learn about your own feelings by how your body and emotions react around a boy. If you're feeling scared, disgusted, or irritated, trust your feelings. You can leave this boy and situation in the dust. You don't need to feel these bad feelings. Or, if you're feeling pleasantly tingly or thrilled, again, trust your feelings. Enjoy the moment and the boy. The biggest word of advice is to trust your feelings. They will give you a clear picture of whether it's a good idea to be in the situation or whether it's time to leave.

Wrap up

Own your feelings and opinions in your relationships. No one needs to be the big boss. Let your friends know how you feel and think and listen to them, too.

Keep track of your own feelings of jealousy and negative thinking. You certainly have the right to all your feelings, but try to work them out and don't take the negative ones out on your friends.

It's absolutely, positively okay to tell a grown-up when you're worried about your friend. You may be giving her the best chance for help that you can.

Enjoy the boys, while you stay in charge of yourself.

Chapter 4

Getting It
ALL DONE

It's Okay to be Smart

Did you know it really is okay to be as smart as you can be? Every girl is smart in her own way. You may be thinking, "I'm not very smart. Everybody else always does better than I do in school." Or, maybe you are super-smart in school, and math and science are easy for you. Some girls are athletes or musicians. Maybe you are a beginning artist, or perhaps you are a really good listener and people like to talk to you. It doesn't matter what "level" or "type" of smart you are, it's okay to be you. Everyone is good at something. What are you good at?

Dear Brave New Girl:

There's so much to keep track of at school. I really try to keep it all straight, but it seems like if I concentrate on studying for my math test, then I get behind in English or I completely forget to do my social studies. Some nights my teachers give me hardly any homework, and other nights they load me up with so much I couldn't get it all done if there were ten of me. Besides, there's other things I want to do at night besides just my homework. There's school dances, sleepovers, church school classes, soccer, swim team—and excuse me, but I'd like to have time to watch a little TV, too. You get the drift. How am I supposed to get everything done?

> SIGNED,
> TOTALLY OVERWHELMED

Dear Totally Overwhelmed:

I'm glad you asked. This is an important question for girls your age. All of a sudden you have so much more to do, more responsibilities, and more activities. Here are some ideas for you.

Keep a homework assignment notebook so you know when tests and quizzes are coming up and when projects are due.

Write all your upcoming events on a calendar so you can look ahead and see what's happening. A calendar will also keep you from scheduling two different things on the same day at the same time.

Try to get most of your homework done before you jump into your play time. Leaving everything until after dinner Sunday night or until a half hour before bed is sure to cause major stress for you. That way, you'll be able to relax and enjoy yourself instead of totally panicking.

When you have a ton of stuff to do, make a list of what you need to do, putting the most important thing first and the least important thing last. Then put a check or a bright-colored doodle next to each "job" as you complete it.

Don't put things off. When you get an assignment on Monday that's not due until Thursday, it's really tempting to let it go, telling yourself, "I'll work on it tomorrow. I have plenty of time." The problem is you'll have stuff to do tomorrow and more on Wednesday, too. Spend a few minutes working on your assignment over the three days you have to get it done. Getting started on your assignment on Monday means that you won't have so much left to do the next two days. Completing it by Thursday will be a breeze.

Reward yourself when you're finished. Give yourself a little treat, such as a bubble bath, a snack, curl up with your favorite book or magazine, or whatever you just love to do.

Be sure and read the rest of this chapter, Totally Overwhelmed. I'll bet you'll find a few more tricks that will help you with everything from keeping your room picked up (at least a little) to finishing your homework to finding time to relax and enjoy yourself, every single day.

Some girls learn things quickly, while others have to work hard, read everything three times, and do the homework to understand. Everybody learns in her own way and in her own time. Let's figure out how you learn best!

Check the statements that are true for you:

____ 1. When I'm learning something new, I like to get right in there and get my hands on it.

____ 2. When I hear the instructions once, I'm usually able to jump right into the project.

____ 3. My friends often call me after school for help with the written homework assignment. They know I always seem to "get it" just by reading the instructions.

____ 4. If I can just sit and think about a project or an assignment for a few minutes, I can usually come up with a pretty cool idea about how to get it done without too much hassle.

____ 5. I bet it will turn out best if you let me do it my way.

____ 6. Let me get my hands on it. I can fix just about anything (you should see me get knots out of shoelaces and necklaces)!

____ 7. I love to read.

____ 8. I prefer ACTION!

____ 9. Even if my teacher hands out instructions for a homework project, everything always make more sense after it's explained to me.

____10. I love to lay around on my bed and dream up neat ideas that no one else has ever thought of.

____11. I wish people wouldn't tell me what to do. I can come up with great ideas about what should be done all by myself.

____12. Learning a foreign language is really easy for me. I seem to be able to repeat what I hear on tapes or from the teacher without any trouble.

____13. I come up with the best ideas when I daydream, and they really work!

____14. Projects go best for me if I can plan ahead and figure out how I'm going to do things.

____15. If I take a good, long look at something, I can remember exactly how it looked—even a week later.

If you checked 1, 6, and 8, you might be a "hands-on" kind of girl. You kind of like things "in your face." You like to touch stuff—get your hands on the merchandise, so to speak. You're an active, let-me-at-it sort of girl. You like to feel, taste, touch, and experience life. This is a great way to live. But don't forget to use your eyes and ears to help you remember the important stuff.

If you checked 2, 9, and 12, you might be a "tell me once and I've got it" sort of girl. You are amazingly able to remember what you are told. Once someone says something to you, it's locked in your brain forever. You hardly ever forget. Just don't try to remember and keep track of everything in your head. You might want to write a list of your assignments or use the calendar to keep track of future events. That way, you won't overload your brain by trying to remember millions of details.

If you checked 3, 7, and 15, you might be a "show me how" or "let me read the instructions" kind of girl. You learn by looking at something or reading it. Once you see the instructions or how something works, you've got it mastered. If you can read about it, you can remember it. You might also want to train your ears and hands to help you. When you hear directions, sometimes you have to use your hands as well as your eyes and brain.

If you checked 4, 10, 13, and 14, you might be a "let me think about it" kind of girl. You work best when you have a few minutes to think things over. You prefer to plan things out and decide how you want to move ahead. You don't like jumping into new things. The downside? Sometimes you wait too long and have a hard time getting started. Try to plan a few steps ahead and then make your move to start your project.

If you checked 5 and 11, you might be a "try it my own way" kind of girl. You detest being told what to do or how to do something. You would always rather try to figure it out yourself. You're convinced that your way is better. This is a strong and confident way to live. The possible problem? Don't get stuck or mad when you have to do something someone else's way. Another way or idea might be great, too, and you could learn new and creative things by trying out another person's idea.

Tips & Tricks for Getting Things DONE

Speak Up, Speak OUT!

When you have to give a speech or presentation, be brave and dig in. It's scary at first just thinking about getting up and talking in front of everyone. But just think, everyone has to be quiet and listen to what you have to say for once! Being in charge is fun. When you have to talk, give a speech, or present your project, you have a great chance to learn to be self-confident. Be sure and ask your parents to help you prepare.

Speeches and projects are important because they let you say what you think, and give you a chance to practice announcing your ideas and the information you have collected. An important part of being confident is learning how to tell the world about yourself and your ideas. Each time you do, you will have more confidence built up for the next time. You may think you should be quiet and let someone else do the talking—not! Your opinion and smarts are just as important as anyone else's.

You know what's really fun? Have someone videotape your presentation. If your family has a video camera, ask a parent to tape you while you practice

your presentation. It's neat to watch yourself on your own television, and you will learn a ton about yourself and how you look and sound while presenting.

Up in Front

There are lots of things you can do to help yourself feel confident at school. Try to position your desk so you can see what's going on and be part of the action. If you go to a special presentation or on a field trip, try to stay close to the front. Usually your teacher gives you a worksheet to fill out, and being close to the action helps you get all the information. Figuring out the answers and being able to report back everything you learned helps you feel smart and confident!

Try to answer all the questions you can. Take every chance you have to go up to the board and write the answers or give information. Besides, your teacher will be terribly impressed.

Studying for Tests and Quizzes

Patrice rolled her eyes. She had studied all night for this test and she barely passed it! And last week, she really blew her quiz in health class. "What's going on?" she wondered. "What more can I do? I know I forgot my notebook in my locker last night, but I read the chapter, all of it. Isn't my brain working or what?"

No wonder Patrice is frustrated. Here she studied for three hours for a test and just barely squeaked by. And her quiz was a disaster! She wondered if her parents were going to be mad.

HAS THIS EVER HAPPENED TO YOU?

Here are some easy tips for studying for tests and quizzes that will help you bring those old grades up:

Highlight. If you own your schoolbooks, use a bright-colored highlighter or marker to call your attention to the important facts. If you don't own your books, quickly jot the important stuff down on a piece of notebook paper with the page number listed after it so you can quickly find it again. You can use this as a study guide for tests.

Read the fine print. Always read all the material assigned, including the captions underneath the pictures, graphs, and charts on each page (that's one I finally learned to do myself, and it's surprising how many test questions come from pictures and graphs in the chapter).

Know the study sheets. If your teacher gives you a study sheet, learn and memorize everything on it. Anything on a study sheet is a big clue about what will probably be on the test or quiz.

Always go for the extra-credit questions or points. That way if you blow a few questions on the test, you can probably make it up in the extra-credit section.

Participate in class. Most teachers give points for class participation. Besides, you learn a ton more when you're paying attention, and class is more interesting when you're adding your own thoughts, feelings, and opinions.

Grill. Ask your parents or call a friend to "grill" you on the questions. Have them ask you each and every question on the study guide sheet, or page through the chapter or your class notes and throw out questions for you to answer. No peeking now!

Write down key words to remember. Finding them in the chapter, writing them down, and having someone "test" you on them is a great way to really learn the material.

Quickly read over all the material before you go to sleep. And speaking of sleep—get a good night's sleep before the test, not during the test! A clear and well-rested brain helps you do your best.

Relax. Before you pick up your pencil to take the test, take three deep breaths, the kind that make your stomach go in and out. Wiggle around to get comfortable and give yourself a positive message about how you will be doing your best.

Learn. Last but not least, remember that getting a good grade is not the only important thing, it's the whole idea of learning that really matters. As long as you learn something and stretch your brain as far as you can, you've done a good job.

CONGRATULATIONS!
Congratulate yourself for a job well done.

Patrice decided to try these ideas out for herself, to see if they worked, on her next test. First, as soon as she heard about the upcoming test in social studies, she got her book out. She figured out that if she studied a little bit each night, it wouldn't seem so overwhelming a day or two before the big event.

So, because she could write in her books, she got out her trusty highlighter and marked the important facts and dates. (If she couldn't write in her book, she could have made notes on a piece of notebook paper.) Then she made sure she read the captions under the pictures and sidebars (the interesting facts along the side of the page).

Next she took time to fill in all (not just the ones that were easy to find and answer, but all) the clues listed on the study sheet her teacher had handed out. She even did a little extra work so she would have some added info for bonus points. She also made a special point to speak up in class, answer questions, and be part of the discussion. She knew her social studies teacher gave extra points for class participation.

Then, for three nights before the test, she asked her parents and her older sister to grill her, asking her all the questions, definitions, and key words off the study sheet in a random order (to trick her!). The night before the test, she went quickly and easily over everything one last time before taking a delicious bubble bath and reading her favorite mystery book for a few minutes. When test time arrived, she knew she had it aced. Although she was a little nervous because it was test day, she was basically able to relax, knowing this was simply a learning challenge and not the end of the world. She knew she would miss a few questions, but this didn't freak her out because she knew almost all the material.

Afterward, she breezed through her day, telling herself she had done all she could. When she got her test results back, she grinned the grin of a winner! Success was hers. Why? Because she had prepared, gotten help, and worked slowly but steadily toward her goal. Go, Patrice!

You are absolutely, positively all right just the way you are. You don't need to do super fabulously good on everything.

Getting Projects Organized

Having a grown-up help you set up your work is helpful. You don't have to figure out your school work alone; your parents and teachers are there to help you. If they act like they're too busy, tell them that this is important to you.

1. First things first. Get the scoop from your teacher about what the project is all about and what is expected of you.

2. Make up a "timeline" for when each part of the project needs to be done, such as the research and the first draft, the hands-on stuff (like pictures, maps, and graphs), and then the final draft. Write these dates down.

3. Figure out what important points you want to say or include. Write them down in the right order.

4. Fill in each important point with lots of information and/or pictures.

5. If you're giving a presentation, practice everything you want to say. Talk out loud in front of your mirror, with a friend, in front of your family, or have someone videotape you giving your presentation or explaining your project.

Rachel got her social studies project assignment on Monday morning. Her teacher said everything would be due in three weeks—Friday the 17th, to be exact. The project had five separate sections to it. Some parts were part of a small group project to be done at school and some parts were to be done by each student at home. "Piece of cake," thought Rachel. "No problem. I can get this done on time. I'll just go to the library during class or flex-time and get the books I need, and I'll be done in no time." Rachel was so sure of herself that she didn't get started on the project right away. Toward the end of the first week, she realized her friends had gotten a good start already. "I'll jump on it right after lunch period on Monday," she told herself. Well, Monday came and went. Rachel had a serious science test Wednesday and she decided she had better hit the books and memorize the review sheet her science teacher had given them to study. "Not to worry about my social studies project, I still have tons of time," she rather nervously told herself.

Guess what happened? The closer the due date got, the more reasons Rachel found not to get started on her project. You would think she would be racing around to get it done, but instead she was starting to panic and pushed it out of her mind. By Thursday night, Rachel had only gotten the parts done that they did in class as small groups. She was so crabby and upset that her mother insisted on knowing why. When Rachel told her mother what had happened, she wasn't too thrilled, as you can imagine. But her mother was willing to help. Rachel cried and knew she had blown it. But what could she do now, the night before?

What Do You Think?

Rachel could:

a. Hide in her closet for the rest of the school year and refuse to come out except to eat and go to the bathroom.

b. Have her mother call her teacher and try to get her off the hook.

c. Come up with a plan for finishing the project and turning it in late. Write her proposal down, sign it (have her mom sign it, too), and talk over her plan tomorrow at school with the teacher.

d. Allow herself to quit, give up, and fail social studies because of one mistake (big though it was).

e. Try to act cool, like she didn't care, and let the chips fall where they may.

What Would You Do?

Let's say you have a gigantic project coming up—one that has many parts (like a report with a presentation) and is due in three weeks. Being the clever girl that you are, write down the steps you would take, starting from first getting the project to turning it in, totally complete, on the exact day it's due.

HERE ARE SOME THINGS TO THINK ABOUT FIRST:

How much time would you need to spend on your project each day?

HOURS   MINUTES

Put a star next to the parts you can do in school and an "X" by the parts you have to work on alone.

Where will you get your information? The library? On the computer? By interviewing someone? Magazines or newspapers?

What supplies will you need? Old magazines to clip out pictures? An encyclopedia? Colored paper, pencils, markers, cardboard, poster board? Folders to keep everything organized? Notecards?

What is your end product going to look like? A typed report? A class presentation? A group of interesting things such as a map, a collage, a puzzle, or a booklet?

Let's see what your plan will be to start and finish your project in perfect time:

1.

2.

3.

4.

5.

There, you did it. You organized your next project. Aren't you proud of yourself? Be sure you notice how you feel this time around. This time you were organized—you planned ahead. I bet you felt better, more calm and in control this time. No more last-minute rushing. No more half-done assignments. Success!

TIME *Eaters*

TICKTICKTICKTICKTICKTICKTICKTICKTICK

Krystal had the best intentions. She planned on doing all her homework, cleaning the bird cage, and practicing her flute before she went to bed that night. But first the phone rang and she just had to talk to Emily, who had just had a big fight with Ashley. That took twenty-five minutes. Then her mother called her for dinner (which just happened to be her favorite), then she had to do her usual clean-up-the-dishes routine. After that, she ran to the store with her dad, since she figured she still had plenty of time to get everything done. Last but certainly not least, her all-time favorite TV show was on at 8:30 P.M. Her mom asked her if all her homework was done and Krystal fibbed and said, "Yes—well, almost . . . ." Of course, her mom said, "No TV until all your homework is done." Krystal was mad at her mom, but most of all, she was mad at herself. "Why didn't I just get it done after school?" she mumbled to herself. "Now I'm missing my favorite show."

Krystal discovered what we all run into from time to time. Even our best intentions to get things done get chewed up by time eaters that seem to eat our time away without our even noticing it. What are some of the worst time eaters?

Did you know that the average kid watches 21 hours of TV per week?* Yikes! TV is eating the brains of you and your friends without you even knowing it. TV gobbles up your time and leaves you with nothing for yourself—no time to read, talk to friends, listen to music, play sports, get to sleep. What would you say to limiting your TV viewing to no more than six hours a week? Yup, six hours, max. Think of all the cool things you could do with your extra time. Write out your TV schedule for the week and stick to it. You don't have to miss your all-time favorite shows. Just turn the TV off the rest of the time. It's not the real world and it's feeding your brain a lot of yukky messages that aren't even true. Pick your shows wisely. Use your brain. You can do this.

*Harris Poll 1995 as cited in *Social Systems, Girls, and Self Esteem*, Minnesota Women's Fund, October 1995.

Shows I Really Want to Watch
Up to Six Hours Per Week

DAY   SHOW   TIME

Sunday

Monday

Tuesday

Wednesday

Thursday

Friday

Saturday

TICKTICKTICKTICKTICKTICKTICKTICKTICKTICKTICKTICKTICK

THE TELEPHONE

Seriously overdoing the telephone can really chew up your time. There is nothing wrong with hanging out on the phone with your friends, it's just that it's pretty easy to end up with the phone glued to your ear from the time you get home to the time to you go to bed. Your parents might already be yapping at you about getting off the phone.

Dinging Around

There's nothing wrong with some good dinging around . . . daydreaming . . . listening to tunes . . . rearranging your dresser drawer with all your hair supplies in it. It's fun and relaxing to hang around and not do anything. In fact, I strongly recommend that you build time into your schedule every day to ding around. But left unchecked, it can eat up your entire evening. It's true your CDs are completely in order (alphabetical, to be precise), and you made a great batch of chocolate chip cookies, and your hair is clean. So what's the problem? Your homework isn't done, that's what. Uh, oh. You've frittered away the entire night.

Worries and Upsets

Worries and upsetting feelings can drain your energy. Try to talk out your problem with someone who can help (a parent, a teacher, or a grandparent). Talking about problems helps you solve them a lot quicker and you don't have to carry them around in your mind and heart. Problems really drag you down and keep you from having the happiness and energy you need to get through your day.

Shopping

It's fun, it's exciting—it's incredibly time consuming. It's so easy to slide through an entire afternoon just window shopping at the mall. Of course there's nothing wrong with shopping, but be careful not to give up every weekend afternoon (as well as all your cash) to the bright lights of the stores.

MOVIES, VIDEOS, ELECTRONIC GAMES

You can lose a ton of time watching little electronic figures zoom around tiny TV screens. These games are really addictive! You tell yourself, "Just one more game . . . just a few more minutes . . . I've almost got it . . . " (You know what I mean.)

TICKTICKTICKTICKTICKTICKTICKTICKTICKTICKTICKTICKTICK

INTERNET

Surfing the internet is fascinating, don't you think? It's important, though, to remember that your parents are paying for Internet time every month. The Internet is not free. Besides the money, you need to watch the clock, because once you start cruising around from subject to subject, it's hard to stop. Give yourself a certain amount of time to surf and read, then STOP. Set a little egg timer or your radio alarm to remind you when its time to quit.

YOUR ROOM—
Castle or **Garbage Dump?**

Besides your homework, you probably have some household chores to do. For most girls, your chores probably are things like picking up your room a little, doing the dinner dishes, cleaning bathrooms, sorting laundry, that sort of thing. You have to get all that done on top of everything else you'd really rather be doing. As a matter of fact, you would probably rather be doing just about anything instead of household chores.

Well, facts are facts. You probably need to do a few things around the house just because you live there and things get messy. How can you get this stuff done with the least amount of time and energy?

Make a list of everything you have to get done each week. Put the list up on your bulletin board (or door, wall, or mirror). Check chores off when you complete them. Ask your parents if you can get paid to do some of these jobs (read Chapter 8 carefully!). A little extra cash can make a job seem a lot easier.

Do something on your job list every single day. Spending a few minutes every day on your chores can keep your room, desk, bathroom, closet, etc. cleaner than you ever imagined. Besides, then you aren't stuck doing everything on Saturday morning. Who wants to spend a whole Saturday cleaning and dusting?

Plenty of girls detest cleaning. These girls love to create, have fabulous ideas, make major messes, and then just don't seem to get around to cleaning them up. You'd rather roar off to your next interesting idea or project than take time to clean up carpets, bedrooms, or kitchen tables. So think about this: What if you gave yourself five, eight, or ten minutes tops to clean, and then you're free? Things don't have to be perfect, but do as much as you can in those few minutes. Then do the rest at the end of the day or with your weekly clean-up.

Make a list of what you have to get done. Decide how many minutes it's going to take you to do each thing, such as:

1. Make my bed: 2 minutes

2. Clean out my hamster cage: 10 minutes

3. Vacuum my room: 3 minutes

Then get a little egg timer and set the timer for each task. It's fun, it's fast, it's easy!

Castle Maintenance

Someday you are going to be in charge of your own castle. Whether it's an apartment, house, cabin in the woods, or mansion, you will be amazed at the number of "repairs" you will have to do to keep it in shape. Lawns need to be mowed, snow shoveled, leaves raked, light bulbs changed, windows repaired, oil changed in cars, walls painted, cupboard doors tightened—the list is endless. So what does this have to do with you, you're wondering? Everything! Remember, someday it's all going to be up to you. Learning how to do some of these things now will make them seem simple when the time comes to do them yourself. You don't want to sit around and have to wait for someone else to rescue you and do your jobs for you. First of all, there may not be anyone; second, it may end up costing you a ton of money; and third, you're perfectly able to do this stuff yourself!

STRESS BUSTERS

You don't have to do everything.

You don't have to get everything done.

YOU DON'T HAVE TO FINISH EVERYTHING PERFECTLY.

Sometimes, you don't even need to do your best—
you only have to do what you can do.

KEEP YOUR SANITY.

LISTEN TO YOUR BODY. IF YOU'RE TIRED, SLEEP. IF YOU'RE RESTLESS, TAKE A BREAK.

Take life one day at a time.
Just do what you can today—no more, no less.

Give yourself time to be nice to yourself: a bubble bath, a long talk on the phone, reading a book by your favorite author, time to daydream. You'll feel better.

If you're overloaded, dump some of the stressful things you're trying to get done. Or do them later when you feel up to it.

The Stressful Side of "Perfectionism"

All these girls are perfectionists. They aren't relaxed and happy unless everything is going completely "right." They want everything in their life to be the best it can possibly be. There's nothing wrong with striving for excellence, but if it completely stresses you out, what's the point?

Letting yourself relax and chill out helps you get things done with greater ease and enjoyment.

You don't have to get the highest grade on every quiz, project, and test. It's okay to be "normal" and "average."

You are perfectly, wonderfully okay just the way you are, mistakes and all.

Remember, you don't have to be perfect; you don't even have to do your best all the time. Sometimes all you need to do is what you can, and that's enough.

Suzanne gets upset when her project doesn't turn out "right."

Serene goes nuts when her room doesn't look "just so."

Sandy detests it when something unexpected happens and she has to change her plans.

Abby feels completely overwhelmed when she has a lot of homework and feels she can't get it organized.

Betsy's stomach churns whenever she has to take a quiz or test because she is so obsessed with getting a high grade. She makes her self sick with worry.

WORD FIND

ORGANIZE	HOMEWORK
LIST	CHORES
ASSIGNMENT	PROJECT
TEST	QUIZ
SPEECH	CLEAN
TIME EATERS	PLAN

```
K  J  K  R  O  W  E  M  O  H  J  Z
O  R  G  A  L  I  C  T  U  O  Z  Y
P  L  A  N  I  S  H  L  Z  U  I  Q
P  R  S  P  S  P  O  K  E  Z  Q  T
P  E  O  K  T  J  R  L  M  D  X  V
C  N  T  I  M  E  E  A  T  E  R  S
K  A  E  E  B  F  S  P  E  E  C  H
S  E  S  W  S  T  C  E  J  O  R  P
N  L  O  X  Q  T  A  I  J  L  E  C
H  C  A  S  S  I  G  N  M  E  N  T
E  Z  I  N  A  G  R  O  B  O  O  M
```

Chapter 5

It's a BiG WoRLd OuT tHERe

Where Do I Fit In?

Dear Brave New Girl:

I hear about bad stuff happening to people on TV, and at school the other day we were talking about homeless people. Last week, someone came out to our church and talked about the families with little kids that don't have enough food and clothing. I know I complain a lot, but I guess I'm really lucky to have as much as I do. Is there anything my friends and I can do to help?

> Signed,
> Wants to Help

Dear Wants to Help:

Wow, am I glad you asked. Why? Because so many people, as well as the Earth, can use all the help they can get. You and your friends can do a lot to help. It's not just up to the adults. So roll up your sleeves and get to it! Here are some ideas to get you started.

Read the totally cool story about Kristen Belanger following this chapter. It's a must-read and will give you tons of ideas and inspiration.

Be active in clothing and food drives at your church or school. Every little bit counts. Search your closet for nice clothes that you don't wear anymore. And tag along to the grocery store with your parents to pick out items to give to the food shelves (good stuff that you'd like to have yourself). Many schools have bins by the office for collecting food.

Volunteer at homeless shelters and food kitchens. How? Have your parents help you look up the phone numbers and give them a call. Many churches and community centers also house and feed homeless adults and kids. These places appreciate having kids come in to help play with and entertain the homeless youngsters who are staying at the shelter.

Send money. Find a jar with a cover, and pop some change into your "sharing jar" every time you get your allowance. At the end of the year or maybe on your birthday, empty your jar and send the money to a special organization that seems important to you. You might pick an organization that protects animals and plants, a group that trains seeing-eye dogs, or a shelter for homeless kids—anything you've heard or read about that touches your heart.

Help clean up your planet. Recycle. Pick up every piece of litter you see when you're walking around outside. You can help make our world look better, brighter, and cleaner with just a minute or two of your time and energy. Go, girls!

LAUREN & ABBY TAKE ACTION!

Lauren and Abby decided to do some serious volunteer work over the summer. They talked to their other friends about it and gathered together eight girls who wanted to be part of their club. They decided to meet once a week and think of things they could do for others and the world during their summer break. They decided this giving/sharing/volunteering would be separate from the "work things" they planned to do to help earn some money for themselves. They popped some popcorn, poured some pop, and sat down in a circle to make a list of possible activities. Here's what they came up with:

✗ Do yard work for someone who has a hard time getting around.

✗ Clean houses/yards/garages/attics for elderly neighbors.

✗ Bake some goodies and bring them to an elderly neighbor or someone in the neighborhood who may have been ill for a long time.

✗ Pick up litter around the neighborhood.

✗ Collect used clothes and bring them to a church or shelter.

✗ Collect mittens, scarves, hats, and coats and bring them to a homeless shelter in the fall.

✗ "Adopt" a family in need for the holidays. Bring them food, gifts, and friendship.

✗ Coordinate a program around the holidays to give toys to kids who might not get anything for the holidays.

✗ Collect canned food for homeless shelters, battered women's shelters, and inner-city community centers and churches.

✗ Volunteer at nursery schools, hospitals, and other places.

Talk things over with your friends and come up with your own ideas. Work projects can be a blast. The dirt under your fingernails and paint in your hair are the "medals of honor" you will receive for a job well done and so much appreciated.

The ABCs of Joining Up and Making Noise

Besides helping out with some of the world's big problems, you can have some fun and also feel like you belong by joining up with other girls on the move. Joining teams, groups, and activities livens up your world. Check out A through Z:

Andrea was a nature girl who helped plant trees and weed garden areas at the local arboretum.

Becca volunteered over summer break at the community center.

Chelsea helped out at the school carnival.

DeeDee was a star on the debate team.

Ellie put her energy in high gear by going on working vacations with her dad. They did community projects like painting community centers, fixing and cleaning up an old house, and washing windows.

Frannie used her free time to join the French Club after school.

Greta grew her own garden. She kept it weeded and watered and shared her veggies and flowers with her family.

Heidi helped out by collecting old books to donate to homeless shelters and inner-city nurseries.

Irene trained for an ice-skating competition.

Josie joined her friends on the junior high fun nights at her church.

Kimmy adored going to Korean Culture Camp.

Lydia learned a lot during her week at Spanish Language Camp.

Maggie memorized her speech for the Mothers and Daughters Luncheon.

Natalie volunteered one Sunday a month at the church nursery.

Olivia wanted to be an orthopedic surgeon someday, so she volunteered at a local hospital four hours a week.

Penny was proud to say she wanted to be a professional chef someday, so each month she took a Kids in the Kitchen cooking class.

Quilla helped an elderly neighbor woman down the block feel like Queen For a Day by bringing her a fresh bouquet of flowers, then helping her with a few chores around her home.

Rhonda made it a point to remember the new kids at school, in the neighborhood, or on her sports team. She always asked them to join in.

Sherry loved to play slow-pitch softball every spring and went swimming every chance she got.

Tanya signed up to be in the sixth grade talent show. She played a mean trumpet solo.

Ulla's parents taught at the university. She loved hearing about colleges and even went to some of the plays and sports events there.

Vicki has been taking voice lessons for three years and can really belt out a tune.

Wanda always went to work with her mom on Take Our Daughters to Work Day.

Xenie wrote a letter every month to TV and movie companies protesting X-rated movies and how they hurt women.

Yolanda took yoga classes at the YWCA.

Zena learned about animals at the local zoo's day camp program.

A Real Girl Story

ROSEMARY'S WORKING VACATION

My name is Rosemary Shultz. When I was eleven years old, I went on vacation with my dad and six people who were going to college at the University of Miami. We were on Spring Break. Spring Break sounds like fun in the sun while you're in Florida, but we were on an "Alternative Spring Break."

I flew to Florida and stayed with my dad. One morning we left his apartment at 4:30 A.M. (yuck). We got into a big van with a few college students, who were nice and very friendly. They talked to me in the van so I wasn't bored. We drove and drove for what seemed like twenty days, but it was really twenty hours until we got there. Where? Tennessee.

First we had a bunch of meetings, then we started working on a church and a house. We scraped all the old paint off and painted on the outside, and we helped inside doing all sorts of things. Some of the college students went to help at a nursery school a little ways away.

To our surprise, we got to be on the TV news. The cameras were there for two days and we ended up on TV for three minutes. I'm not kidding!

All our work really paid off. We helped make a house that was full of bugs and had almost nothing in the refrigerator, a lot better. When we left, the house looked like a much brighter and happier place to be. We helped make a community church better and nicer to be in. The preacher there was very grateful for all the things we had done. She was a very friendly and nice person. We had a lot of fun with her. We made a lot of things better and I'm glad we did. I also learned a few things myself. I learned that I should be thankful that I have such a loving family and a nice community to live in. I have very good health. I'm so thankful for everything.

HANDS AND HEADS

Learning to use your hands to do "mechanical" stuff is really important. Boys and men used to take care of all the nuts and bolts activities around the house, while girls and women did the cooking and cleaning. NO MORE! You need to know how to operate the electrical circuit breakers and use a paintbrush, and how to check the oil on the car. You can't sit around and hope that some guy comes along to rescue you from the dirty work.

Take this quiz to see how many things you know how to do:

1. Change a light bulb that blows out
    Yes   No

2. Run the dishwasher
    Yes   No

3. Sort the laundry
    Yes   No

4. Run the washer and dryer
    Yes   No

5. Program the VCR to record a show that will be on later
    Yes   No

6. Flip the circuit breaker if lights or appliances go out
    Yes   No

7. Check the oil level in your family car
    Yes   No

8. Load film in a camera
    Yes   No

9. Run a video camera
    Yes   No

10. Lock and unlock all the doors in the house
    Yes   No

11. Call the right phone numbers for all life-threatening emergencies
    Yes   No

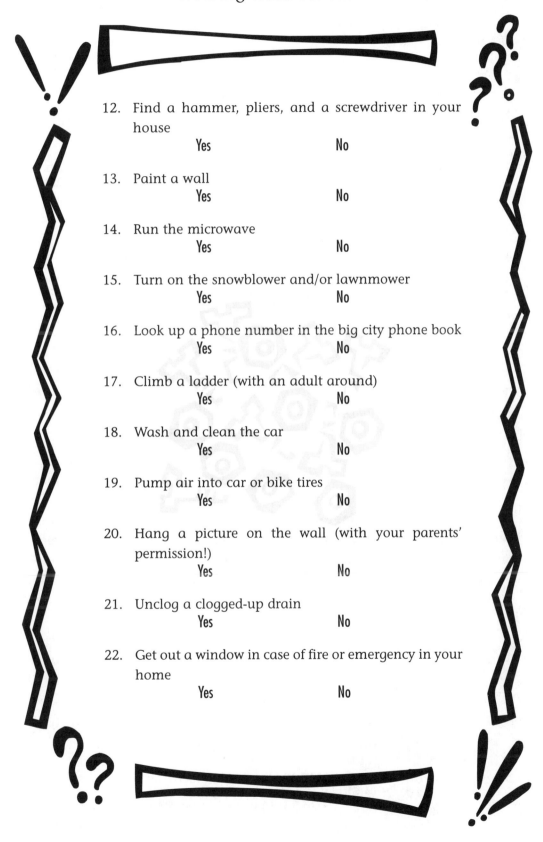

12. Find a hammer, pliers, and a screwdriver in your house

    Yes   No

13. Paint a wall

    Yes   No

14. Run the microwave

    Yes   No

15. Turn on the snowblower and/or lawnmower

    Yes   No

16. Look up a phone number in the big city phone book

    Yes   No

17. Climb a ladder (with an adult around)

    Yes   No

18. Wash and clean the car

    Yes   No

19. Pump air into car or bike tires

    Yes   No

20. Hang a picture on the wall (with your parents' permission!)

    Yes   No

21. Unclog a clogged-up drain

    Yes   No

22. Get out a window in case of fire or emergency in your home

    Yes   No

YOUR SCORE

20–22 YES answers earns you a round of applause. You are well on your way to becoming an independent, self-confident girl and woman.

18–19 YES answers shows you are learning to handle everyday tasks with your head and hands. Keep up the good work!

13–17 YES answers says you are beginning to learn important things about keeping a house/apartment and car glued together. Keep learning everything you can!

12 or fewer YES answers means you should ask your parents to show you how to do these important tasks, and soon you too will be a can-do girl.

BUZZING AROUND

JoJo was totally lost. Her heart was beating a mile a minute. She thought she knew the way to Kit's apartment, but apparently she didn't. She turned left at the first corner, went two blocks, then turned right. She panicked and wondered if she should have turned left. Now she was all turned around. She rode her bike around the block and finally spotted Kit's apartment building with the bright red flowers in front. Thank goodness—what a scare! It took a while for her heart to stop pounding.

What happened to JoJo can happen to anyone. Getting lost really gives you a creepy feeling. It can be frustrating or funny, depending on the situation. You'll want to learn to find your way around so you can safely and easily go to a high school football game and later maybe take a tour of France and Italy. You want to figure out how to get where it is you want to go and, even more importantly, how to get yourself back home again in one piece. Someday you'll be going to airports and exciting new cities all by yourself. You want to learn how to do that a little bit at a time.

Where Am I?

If you think that you can just remember directions to everywhere you go, think again. If you're in a strange new airport or a huge unfamiliar city, "memorizing the way" definitely won't help. Now what?

HERE'S SOME NEAT WAYS TO START LEARNING HOW TO FIGURE OUT WHERE YOU ARE:

Start in your own city or town.

When you take even a tiny trip, check the map in the car and figure out what road you're taking.

Pester your parents with tons of questions when you're going somewhere in the car. Also look for signs that answer these kinds of questions:

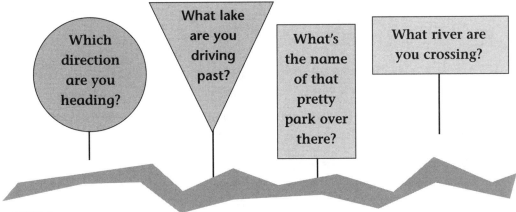

TIPS

Call before you go shopping to find out how late the store is open or if they have the jeans you want in your size.

When you eat in a restaurant, add up the cost of the items everyone ordered to give you an idea about how much a night on the town or a trip might cost.

When you go to an amusement park or a huge event, take one of the maps at the entrance and try to figure out how to get where you want to go, rather than just bumbling along, hoping you can find or remember where everything is.

Pack your own suitcase when you're going somewhere overnight. Be responsible for remembering your own stuff. Don't rely on good ol' Mom to remember your toothbrush and favorite stuffed animal.

If You ◆ *Get Lost*

Remember, even the most organized travelers get lost from time to time.

Don't panic (yet).

If you can, retrace your steps to a familiar place.

Ask for directions. It's best to go into a store or place of business and ask someone who works there. Ask to use the phone, if you can.

Never, never, never, NEVER get into a stranger's car, even if the person offers to take you where you want to go. Never! Run away as fast as you can.

Listen to Your Instincts

Whether you're cruising around, traveling, or just plain lost, it's important to listen to your body. It tends to give you valuable information.

If the hair on the back of your neck is standing straight up, you're probably a little lost. You'd better head back toward familiar territory.

If you have the creepy feeling that you've gotten off at the totally wrong bus stop, stop and figure out the safest route back to safety.

Be aware of how "safe" or "unsafe" you feel. Are people watching you in a weird way? Is it getting too dark outside? Could you get help in stores or businesses?

Try to remember to go places in a group. Being alone is always more dangerous. There is safety in numbers. You're not out there alone, just one small body; you're part of a team.

Now consider Nettie. She had practiced figuring out where she is and how to get to where she's going.

Nettie was at the Mall of America in Bloomington, Minnesota, the absolute biggest shopping mall in the United States. She and her family were visiting relatives nearby, and Nettie was having a great time with her cousins and their friends. Of course, they headed out to the mall at the first chance they had. What a blast! Right in the middle of the mall (which had hundreds of stores—everything you could imagine) was a huge amusement park called Camp Snoopy, with tons of full-sized rides and all kinds of food. Nettie thought she was in heaven.

Everything was going great. They decided to split into two groups and each go off to the stores they wanted, and meet back by the log ride in Camp Snoopy at 2:30. Nettie doesn't know how it happened, but she found herself totally alone in a humongous shopping mall with the sound of the roller coaster roaring in her ears. She wasn't supposed to meet her friends back at Camp Snoopy for almost two more hours. She didn't have the faintest idea where she was, and there were four floors and three hundred stores in this place! Her heart began to pound and she felt like she couldn't swallow.

WHAT SHOULD NETTIE DO?

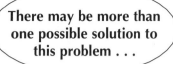

1. Just keep walking. Maybe she'll see her cousins somewhere.

2. Duck into a store and ask to use the phone to call her aunt's house and ask what she should do.

3. Just keep shopping until 2:30 and then head over to Camp Snoopy.

4. Hide out in the bathroom.

5. Ask that group of eighteen-year-olds over by the ice cream stand if they would help.

6. Go up to one of the security guards and ask for help.

7. Retrace her steps and see if maybe they just got separated at the last store. Maybe her friends didn't even realize she was gone.

8. Pass out from sheer fear.

Here's What Might Happen . . .

1. *Just keep walking.* This might work, but probably not. In a gigantic shopping mall, Nettie could walk forever and not find the people she's looking for. Besides, she might get even more lost, if that's possible, which will make her even more scared and panicky.

2. *Duck into a store and call her aunt.* This is a definite possibility. At least Nettie's aunt could come and get her and help her design a plan to find her cousins. Never be afraid to ask salespeople at a store for help. If they're not helpful, ask to speak to a manager. I know that's super-scary, but hey, you can be brave just for a few minutes, anyway. (Note: it's helpful to carry a quarter with you for a pay phone.)

3. *Just keep shopping.* Probably not such a hot idea. Nettie's cousins will be freaking out when they discover she's missing, and they'll probably spend the whole time looking for Nettie.

4. *Hide out in the bathroom.* This may sound like a good idea, but it's pretty hard to be seen or found when you're hiding behind a door in the bathroom. Besides, it really isn't much fun.

5. *Ask a group of eighteen-year-olds for help.* Risky. Very risky. They could be the greatest, sweetest group of kids you could ever imagine. Or, they could be total, absolute, complete creeps. You just don't know. Avoid this one.

6. *Ask the security guards.* Definitely a good plan. They have all kinds of equipment (phones, walkie-talkies, pagers, etc.) to help them locate people anywhere in the shopping mall. Just think, if Nettie's cousins have already talked to a salesperson who has called the security guards, one call from Nettie's security guard and she is home free.

7. *Retrace her steps.* Yes and no. It depends on how long they've been separated. If it's been one or two minutes, this might work. If it's been five or ten minutes, it might not work. Nettie and her cousins are probably too far apart.

8. *Pass out from sheer fear.* Nettie probably feels like this, but she won't really faint. She's just scared. She should slow down and talk calmly to herself about her plan as she heads off for help. Everything will be okay.

Cultural Diversity

We're all a little different. We have different backgrounds and our families celebrate different holidays and events. Being different is neat. Wouldn't it be boring if we all looked and acted exactly the same?

Joining in on an activity is fun. It can be especially cool if it's connected to your cultural heritage. You have a chance to learn about your background—the language, the food, and the special celebrations of your grandparents and great-grandparents.

Home Sweet Home

Here are some ideas to help you feel connected to your family:

Ask if you can have an "heirloom" from your family in your room. An heirloom is a special object that belongs just to your family that your grandparents or great-grandparents or some other older relative owned. This is a treasured item that has been "passed down" and may have been kept in your family for years and years. Some of these items can be a hundred years old and come from the "pioneering" days. You have to be incredibly careful when you handle an heirloom, though, because if it gets broken or lost you can't go to the store and buy another one. Having an heirloom in your room helps you feel like a part of a very long, loving line of people.

Be part of your family celebrations. Help bake the birthday cake, the holiday food, purchase the gifts, and decorate your home. Get in on the good times.

Learn about your cultural heritage. See if your parents can help you attend a camp or event that focuses on your cultural heritage.

Keep a journal or a diary. Write down the story of your life. Keep it forever! Here's a part of Mariel's story:

A Real Girl Story

MARIEL AT KOREAN CULTURE CAMP

Today is a very special day for me because I'm writing about Korean Culture Camp. At camp, we learned all sorts of things. We learned how to talk in the Korean language. For example, how to say "hello" and "how are you" in Korean. One of my teacher's accents showed that she is definitely from Korea. We also learned a really cool dance. It was called the puppet dance. We pretended like we were puppets. That's why it is called the puppet dance. We performed it after working on it all week. The food was quite weird, but after having it for a while, I started to like it. We had mahn-du. It's kind of like an egg roll, which I think is kind of gross, but on the bright side, it's kind of good. My favorite was the noodle stuff. It was sooo good!

I bet you're wondering how I felt. Well, I felt comfortable and I felt uncomfortable. I am used to maybe one to two Koreans around me, but this was really weird! When four hundred people look just like me, I feel a little bit uncomfortable. Sometimes I wanted to go home, but later in the week I started to feel better.

I learned a lot. I had a super-fun time and I want to go back.

Mariel Kim Shultz, age ten, is currently in the fourth grade. She loves music, guinea pigs, creating minibooks, sports, and having fun.

HOW ABOUT YOU?

What nationality are you? (If you're not sure, ask your parents.)

What kinds of foods do you eat for special holidays?

Are there special dishes that you always have because it's "tradition"? What is your favorite one?

Try to go to one event (soon!) that focuses on your cultural heritage. Write about it here:

My Heritage

Team up with your parents or grandparents and get the inside scoop on your cultural heritage. Record your answers here for future reference:

My cultural heritage is:

My grandparents were born in:

My great-grandparents were from:

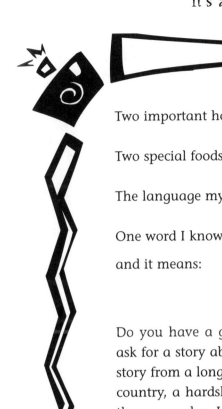

Two important holidays my culture celebrates are:

Two special foods from my cultural heritage are:

The language my ancestors spoke is:

One word I know from that language is:

and it means:

Interview Time

Do you have a grandparent or other relative you could ask for a story about your cultural heritage? Maybe it's a story from a long time ago—about how they came to this country, a hardship they endured, or a huge celebration they remember. Here's your chance to hear and record this story. Take notes and then write it down right here in your book. It will be a really cool reminder of your family roots.

Date: Relative interviewed:

Story I was told:

A Real Girl Story

DOING ALL I CAN

BY KRISTEN BELANGER

I have found throughout my fourteen years on this earth that being a kid isn't the easiest job. Nor is it easy to find healthy self-esteem deep down inside yourself. The nineties are a time of poverty, violence, gangs, and negativity that makes it all the more difficult to become a well-balanced adult. I do admit I have had my troubles growing up, but I have found a few ways to start myself on a path to success and help out the rest of the world, too.

Five years ago, when I was nine years old and in fifth grade, I just happened to be reading a Greenpeace magazine about rainforests. The article emphasized how acres of growth were being chopped down at an incredible rate. I was suddenly moved by all of this. I wanted to help out. I couldn't wait, so I called up my friend Marcy. I told her the idea of having a "Rain Forest Day" at our elementary school in Connecticut. We decided to make up a proposal and present it to our principal.

After a few weeks of meeting with teachers and making plans, our idea evolved into two separate projects. One was raising food for our local food bank and the other was raising money for a local soup kitchen. Marcy and I then motivated kids in our elementary school to do extra chores at home and raise money and bring food to donate. In the end we collected over $700 for the soup kitchen and a truckload of food to stock the food bank.

I was so excited that I couldn't stop. Marcy and I decided to do another project, but this one separate from our school. It was now the summer and deciding what to do was hard. We finally agreed on a clothing drive and immediately pulled together and distributed posters. In our small town, word of mouth was a great source, but we weren't satisfied with only that. I wanted to collect up to 500 pounds of winter clothing. I knew that was a lot, but the ad I put in our local paper helped us on our way. Every day I would pick up clothing that I had arranged to be dropped off by the local townspeople at two selected spots. I would go down in my basement and sort and fold the clothes every night. It was hard work, and sometimes I would much rather have watched Oprah or gone shopping, but I pushed myself and fought off those urges. Now don't get me wrong, I still lived as normal a life as possible. Although sometimes it was hard, I did it to the best of my knowledge.

At the end of my First Annual Winter Clothing Drive, Marcy and I had collected 811 pounds of winter clothing. Not only did I achieve my goal, I went 311 pounds over it. What a feeling that was!

Our next task was to decide on an organization to donate the clothes to. Wait a minute—obstacle #1. No organization near us could handle and distribute 811 pounds of clothes. Through many phone calls and much "red tape," I got in touch with E.A.R.T.H. (Education and Resources to Help), an organization geared to help the Indians of South Dakota. I loved it. An organization that could handle all the clothing and a branch of it was near me. Wait another second—obstacle #2. Marcy didn't believe the Indians were classified as homeless, which is how we had worded our posters. I thought the Indians on the reservations definitely did qualify as needy enough to get the clothes.

I love Marcy dearly as a good friend, but we fought over that for a while. Finally she did agree to donate the clothes to the Indians. I knew in my heart of hearts that these people needed this clothing and winter was coming fast. Over the next months after the hard work of the drive was finally complete, my relationship with Marcy strengthened again. As that happened, we parted and went our separate ways. I was left with the decision of whether to try to do the projects myself. Of course when I say "myself," I am leaving out my family—my mom Lydia, dad David, and sister Jessica—who are a fabulous support system. I thought about it for a while and decided to keep going.

Since the first year of starting to do community projects, I have done many others and run into other obstacles that I have had to tackle. For instance, I can never get the kids in my town to help me, so I do the projects myself with help from my family. In the beginning I had gotten so used to working with Marcy, I wanted other kids to just jump right in. Many of them showed some interest, but backed out when they saw how much work was involved. After a while I gave up trying to solicit their help and I moved on. I was successful and collected more and more clothes each year. I also collected 750 books for children, enough money for an entire Christmas for a Vietnamese family, $1,400 for Christmas toys for kids who had been flooded out of their homes, and most of the stuff a teenage mother would need for her premature baby.

One of the most serious problems I faced was teasing. When I started out on my "mission" five years ago, I never figured that I would get teased about it. After a while I learned that teasing is a way to get control. It puts the person teasing at the top of the totem pole and you at the bottom. It took me a while to figure out that the cure for teasing is to ignore it. Teasers don't find it any fun anymore when they can't stir you up. Then they lose interest, and finally go away or stop.

I have gotten back a lot for the work I have done. I have been in the newspaper, on the radio, and on TV many times. I have won many awards and I have gotten a scholarship for my college education. I have been able to go many places and meet incredible people. Sometimes I get tired of all the attention and I just want to be a "normal kid," but I have had a really interesting life. I have had the chance to change the lives of many people and make the world a little bit better.

One of the most important things for me has been the relationship that I had with a homeless woman. My mom, sister, and I followed her one day after we saw her eating out of a garbage pail. We talked to her and after that we kept visiting her and bringing her things to make her life a little easier. After about a year and a half of that, she found a place to live and got off the street for good. We wrote to each other for a long time after that and she let me know how much the help I gave her meant to her. We see her sometimes now and you would never know that she had been homeless. It made me understand that anyone can be homeless and that even if people have been homeless for a while, they can get themselves back on their feet. I was happy to be able to watch that happen and maybe to have something to do with it happening. When I lecture at schools, I tell other kids about my experience with the homeless woman, but I also tell them never to approach a homeless person without an adult along. It is important to make changes, but it is also important to stay safe.

For myself, I have found that the best way to build self-esteem is to believe in yourself. During times of hardship in your family or with your friends, you may have felt that someone didn't believe in you. I used to feel that way a lot when kids my age didn't understand what I was doing and made fun of me. The way to keep up your self-esteem is to believe in yourself and know that you are a great person and that you are doing your best to grow up. If you can make positive changes in the world along the way, that's even better.

Fourteen-year-old Kristen Belanger has a long list of accomplishments that began when she was only nine years old. She has been profiled on national television shows, including "Gettin' Over" with Tony Danza on ABC and "A Current Affair." She has also won the kids' category in the National Hero Award competition and was a runner-up for the JC Penney Golden Rule Award, which salutes the volunteer spirit. She has been voted into The Giraffe Project, an organization that recognizes people for "sticking their necks out." Only around 750 people have been voted into Giraffes, and Kristen is one of them. Her clothing drives have now collected over 2,300 pounds of warm clothing, and she has raised over $8,000 to donate to those in need.

Chapter 6

My Family & Me

Living with your parents and maybe a brother or sister (or two or three), a guinea pig, two cats, a hamster, goldfish, and a dog can drive any self-respecting girl crazy! What can you do?

TALES OF THE WEIRD
(ALSO KNOWN AS THE STORY OF MY FAMILY)

I am blessed/stuck with ⬤ sisters, ◼ brothers, and ▲ cousins in my family.

The best thing about my family is:

The absolute worst thing about my family is:

The weirdest thing my family does is:

I wish my parents would let me:

91

The Mysterious Case of the DISAPPEARING Privacy

Carrie walked into her room after school one crisp fall day and gasped. Her sister had turned their shared bedroom into a "magical forest" of draped blankets, umbrellas, and pillows. Her sister had even taken Carrie's prized homemade quilt off her bed and draped it across her desk and chair! She sighed and realized that once again all her privacy had completely disappeared. Even before this latest "magic forest" episode, Carrie found that sharing a room with her younger sister was becoming harder and harder. Carrie liked things neat and tidy, but mainly she liked her privacy. Her younger sister was a slob, and noisy on top of it. She was getting frustrated because she wanted to talk on the phone to her friends, or just hang out in her room without her sister intruding. She tried taping a string down the middle of the room to divide the space in half, but the noise, clutter, and interruptions still drove her crazy. She talked it over with her mom, who helped her plan ways to get a moment of peace and quiet. It wasn't perfect, but it was better than nothing.

Here are some of the ideas they came up with to help Carrie feel like she had more privacy:

Use a free-standing room divider (that could also be used as a bulletin board) to split up the room.

Have certain periods of the day when one girl could have thirty minutes of time alone in the room.

Make up a list of "ground rules" that each girl must follow, and post the list on the door.

Neither girl could use her sister's stuff (including clothes, bed, school stuff, bathroom or hair supplies, etc.) without first asking permission.

Assign certain days for each girl to play the music of her choice in the room.

Set aside a few minutes or hours each day for quiet time in the room.

What are some of your ideas?

Privacy = Safety Zones

It's really important to have your own space, isn't it? Your space is where you can do whatever you want without anyone watching over you or telling you what to do. Your space is where you can keep things that are important and special to you. You have the right to some space all to yourself. Maybe it's a whole bedroom, maybe it's your bed or bookshelf, or perhaps simply a box to keep your treasures in. As you get older, you will probably find that you crave more and more privacy. You don't want anyone listening to your telephone conversations or (heaven forbid) reading your poems and stories. You go nuts when anyone marches into your room when you're dressing or goes through your dresser drawers when you're not home. You know what? You're absolutely right. You have a right to your privacy and it's not fair to you when other people invade your space and snoop around.

Dear Brave New Girl:
Every time I'm in the bathroom or even in my own bedroom with the door shut, my little brother and sister just barge in without knocking. I've told my mom how much this bugs me and she tells them not to, but they keep doing it anyway. And then I get in trouble for yelling at them! Do you believe it? My parents always side with those little rugrats. It drives me loony. I can't stand it! I'm old enough to deserve a little privacy, but I don't know how to get it. Help!
     Signed,
     No Privacy

Dear No Privacy:
What a bummer! It sounds likes it's time for a family discussion about privacy. You have a right to privacy and don't have to put up with siblings or grown-ups barging into your room or the bathroom when you're in there.

How do you get the privacy you need?

Call a family meeting. Gather everyone around the kitchen table and bring up your concerns in an honest and straightforward way. Tell your family how you feel and how you would like things to be different.

Suggest that it's time to establish "ground rules" for coming and going into the bathrooms and bedrooms. Have consequences if the rules aren't followed.

rules

Here are a few possible ground rules:

How long do I get in the bathroom?

Do people have to knock before entering my room?

Yes   **No**

Which dresser drawers, bookshelves, etc. are off limits to anyone else?

Can people go in my room when I'm not home?

Yes   **No**

What rules do I have to follow for keeping my personal space clean?

If someone wants to borrow something from my room when I'm gone they will:

Does my brother/sister have to ask my permission to "cut through" my room on the way to another room?

Yes   **No**

Can other people use the phone/radio/CD player in my room when I'm not home?

Yes   **No**

Write up your list of ground rules and have everyone in your home sign it (except your pet fish, of course). Then post it somewhere where it can easily be seen. Change the rules only when they no longer work and need updating. Good luck!

SIBLINGS

Brothers and sisters: you love them and you can't stand them at the same time. They're totally in your way and yet never around when you need them (or when you need something they own). How can a girl possibly live in the same house as a sister who has a freak attack if you touch anything that belongs to her, or a brother who looks at you like you're something he's never seen before from another planet?

Sometimes you get along absolutely great. You have the best time in the world. You laugh and giggle and carry on, totally enjoying being with each other. Then sometimes you can't imagine ever being as furious with another human being as you are with your sib. You cannot—absolutely cannot—believe anyone could be that maddening. You wish you'd never seen or heard of this infuriating person.

Sometimes you whisper together and laugh until you feel dizzy about something really dopey that your parents will never, ever understand. Your parents just look at you like you've lost your mind.

Other times your sibs treat you like dirt. They annoy you, frustrate you, tattle on you, act like they're in charge of you, and just plain bug the daylights out of you.

You love them so much, but you can't stand them half the time.

Dear Brave New Girl:

I need to move to another state. I cannot live with these obnoxious people any longer. I have an older brother and a younger sister. My brother won't let me do anything he does. If his friends are around, he treats me like I'm stupid or like I don't even exist. In short, he treats me like dirt. My little sister follows me around and interrupts every phone call and every sleepover. If I have a friend over, she keeps walking into my room with some dumb excuse that she needs something. My friends think she's cute, but I think she's being rude. I always try to be really nice to both of them and talk to them in a decent tone of voice (as my mother keeps suggesting). But it doesn't make any difference. They just continue to act like they're so important and I'm not. Do you know any family I could go live with without any bratty little kids?

SIGNED,

FED-UP

Dear Fed-Up:

It sounds like you feel like you're stuck with the two worst siblings in the world (and yet, at the same time you know you love them, too). Of course you are going to have a lot of mixed feelings about your brother and sister. That's perfectly natural.

What Can You Do?

It might be helpful if your sister could have a friend sleep over the same night you have someone staying. That way she'll have her own pal.

Talk to your mom and your sister and write up some ground rules for when you have friends over. Include things such as how many times she can come to your room, can she have a snack with you, and can she watch a video with you.

Talk to your parents and have a heart-to-heart talk with your brother about your feelings. Tell him you need to be treated respectfully. But remember not to barge in on him when he's with his friends (you detest it when your little sister does that to you).

Be a great role-model, showing them how you want to be treated by how you treat them.

Good luck! Hopefully, you won't have to move now.

How to Talk to Your Mom and Dad so They Don't Always Say

NO!

You know how it is. You and your friends have cooked up a really good plan to go to the movies. You're in a perfectly good mood and run upstairs to ask your mom if you can go. She asks, "How are you planning to get there, and is an adult going to stay at the theater with you?" You assure her that Gayle's dad is driving you all there, then you ask your mom if she could come pick you up. This immediately clues your mom into the fact that no adult is going to be there, and so she automatically says no without even giving your idea a chance. So, you get mad and the argument begins. Pretty soon, you're both mad and there's no way she is going to say yes and you end up staying home. What a drag. Is there some way to make things go differently next time? Here are some tips.

Know your family rules. When making plans with your friends, take into consideration the rules. Does an adult need to be at the shopping mall, movie theater, or bowling alley with you?

Give your parents tons of information about:

What you're doing

Who's going to be there

What adult is going to be around

What you have to do for school

Where you're going

What your plans are

Who your friends are

Remember that your parents have plenty to do, too. I know a girl who once announced that it was her mother's job to take her where she wanted to go. Not! Your parents were not put on this earth simply to drive you around. They're doing you a favor because they love you and want you to have an enjoyable life. But, it is not, I repeat, not their number one job in life to chauffeur you around.

Try to arrange a carpool. With a carpool ready to go, your parents won't be the only ones driving you and your friends around. They'll appreciate the effort you made to make things easier for them.

Don't do stuff they tell you not to do. This will automatically put you in the doghouse. If they find out that you broke a basic family rule (and it seems like they always do), they won't be able to trust you. And I can guarantee you that if they don't trust you, they won't say yes.

Let your parents meet your friends. (This tip is a biggie.) Have your friends over for sleepovers, for supper, or just to hang out on a Saturday afternoon. The more your parents know about your life and who you hang out with, the more they will let you do the things you want to do. The less the know, they more they will say no because they are not sure what's going to happen or who's going to be there. Trust me on this one; it's the truth.

Remember, it's not necessarily you they don't trust, it's the weird, unsafe people in the world they don't trust. They may not let you go to the mall or movies alone because a few nasty people out there may make your visit unsafe. They trust you; they are just worried about everyone else. Young girls really aren't able to handle weird grown-ups or older adolescents the way a grown-up could. Your parents just want to keep you safe and alive.

Negotiate a change in the rules before you need it. If it is time to consider changing a rule, bring up the idea when you're not trying to get permission to do something new and different. Talk about it ahead of time.

What Do YOU Think the Rules Should Be?

I know, I know. You think kids should be able to sleep until noon, go to school one day a week, have total freedom and no homework, and be able to drive a car when they are eight years old. Have I got it right? In the real world, you probably won't get all those wishes granted. So if you think in terms of the real world and if you could wave the old magic wand, what do you think the rules for you should be? (Be real now!)

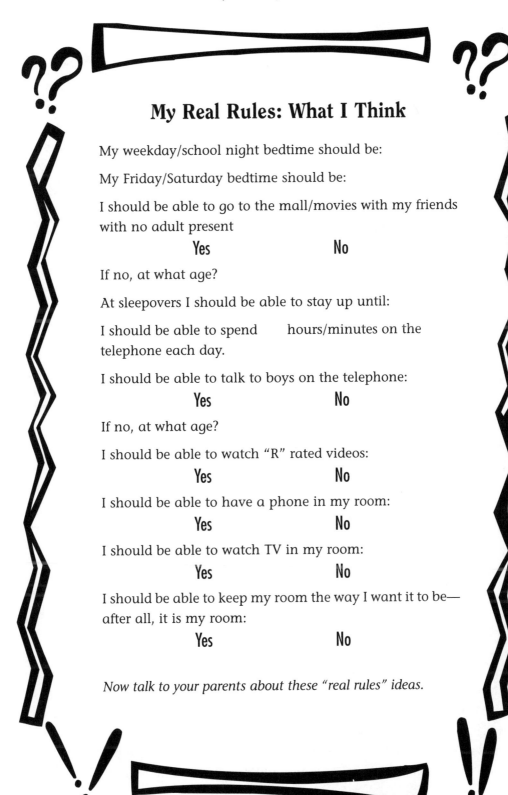

My Real Rules: What I Think

My weekday/school night bedtime should be:

My Friday/Saturday bedtime should be:

I should be able to go to the mall/movies with my friends with no adult present

Yes   **No**

If no, at what age?

At sleepovers I should be able to stay up until:

I should be able to spend   hours/minutes on the telephone each day.

I should be able to talk to boys on the telephone:

Yes   **No**

If no, at what age?

I should be able to watch "R" rated videos:

Yes   **No**

I should be able to have a phone in my room:

Yes   **No**

I should be able to watch TV in my room:

Yes   **No**

I should be able to keep my room the way I want it to be—after all, it is my room:

Yes   **No**

Now talk to your parents about these "real rules" ideas.

When to Talk it Over with Your Parents

You don't have to do this thing called life alone. Reach out. Life is a "we" thing.

Obviously, you don't feel like telling your parents every little thing. I mean, a girl needs her privacy, right? It's great to share your ups and downs and worries and triumphs with your friends. But sometimes you need someone older and perhaps wiser to help you know what to do or where to turn. You need some real, genuine comfort. You need a parent or a grown-up.

Grown-up friends, parents, teachers, coaches, relatives, and neighbors are truly there to help you. Reach out and talk to them. They may seem hopelessly out of date, or you may be convinced that they don't understand you or know what they're talking about, but trust me on this one—these people can help you figure out this life stuff.

IT MIGHT BE TIME TO TALK TO A GROWN-UP WHEN:

you want help puzzling out your options and solutions.

anyone physically hurts or threatens you, or gives you the serious creeps.

you feel hurt or afraid—even if the hurt and fears seem silly. Your feelings and worries are never, ever silly. Often a grown-up can help you see a better solution or can reassure you that you're going to be okay.

YOU FEEL ANXIOUS, DEPRESSED, WORRIED, OR FREAKED OUT.

you want a hug, some encouragement, or a little conversation.

you're in big, big trouble and you know it.

you don't feel loved or appreciated.

Life can get pretty messy and complicated. It's a great idea to turn to the grown-ups in your life to help you over the bumps. You never have to try to figure things out for yourself or be alone with your problems. Adults (as you have already figured out) certainly don't know everything, but it's nice to have someone to lean on and to give support, love, and a helping hand. Life is too complicated to try to do it alone. It's so much easier to have help along the way.

NOT FAIR!

Dear Brave New Girl:

My parents are so strict. You wouldn't believe it. All my friends get to stay up as late as they want, even on school nights. And they get to watch whatever they want on TV and do fun things with their friends on the weekend. My parents make me do my homework first, get to bed by 9:30 P.M. (do you believe it?!) and always tell them where I'm going. How should I know what we're going to decide to do? Maybe we'll get to Nikki's house and then decide to run over to the mall. I can't know what every-one's going to want to do. And I know my mother reads my diary. I told her it's pri-vate and I try to hide it, but she's such a snoop. And last, boys—my parents won't let me go out with them. I can barely talk to them on the phone. My dad says I can see Jason at school and that's enough. Not fair! Not fair, I say. (By the way, I'm almost thirteen and in seventh grade.)

    SIGNED,

    NOT FAIR

Dear Not Fair:

You've brought up a couple of really good points. You're right, parents aren't always fair and yet, you're stuck with them.

First, you are indeed right in saying your diary is private—off limits! Your mom doesn't have the right to snoop and read your private stuff (letters, diaries, journals, and personal notes). You might want to talk to your mom and bring this book along to show her. However, if your mom truly thinks you're doing something really scary (like drugs), she may need to get all the info she can, including from your private stash. But, unless she really, really, really needs to keep tabs on what you're doing, everyone needs to stay out, out, out of your private papers.

You can negotiate your bedtime with your parents, but most important is to pay attention to what your body needs. Everybody is different. Some girls need lots of sleep to function their best and others get by on not much at all. Some girls need to have all ten toes in bed much earlier than their friends in order to stay healthy and bright-eyed. Your mom probably sees that you need your sleep or else your body has a fit. Try to negotiate a later time on week-ends and holidays.

Parents just love knowing where their kids are. It gives them a little sense of security. They're not so much afraid to trust you, it's all the other nutty peo-ple roaming around that worry them. They want you to live a long and healthy life. Pamper them by letting them know where you're going. (Here's a hint: they'll probably let you do more if you let them know what's going on.)

Boys? Parents are supposed to freak out about boys being interested in their daughters. It's their job. Humor them and play it slow and safe. Don't sneak around behind their backs; it will just make them think you're doing even more stuff you're not supposed to be doing. Get to know boys in a casual, easy way at school, on the phone, in large groups. Have fun while moving at your own pace and not rushing ahead.

Fun With my **FAMILY?**

I guess this isn't so bad . . .

"Enjoy my family?" you squeal. "You've got to be kidding. Oh, pulllllleeease!" Yes, enjoy them. What a concept, huh? Think about it—since you're stuck with your family, you'd might as well enjoy them from time to time. How can you get the most enjoyment out of having to live with them? There are quite a few fun things you can do with these altogether strange people, even your siblings and parents.

Have sleepovers at your house. That way your parents can meet your friends (hint, hint) without getting in your hair (too much). Decide ahead of time on a bedtime, snacks, and which videos to get so there's no unexpected problems popping up.

Get your family motivated and go bowling, skating, swimming, or do something active. You'll all feel better and work up an appetite. Then . . .

Make a fun meal together. Plan a barbeque (even in the middle of the winter), a picnic, a homemade pizza, a fancy candlelight dinner, a special ethnic dish. Food is fun. You might as well enjoy preparing it, too.

Rent an old movie. Your parents will love it and you will be surprised at how good it really is. You'll probably end up telling your friends they simply have to see it next weekend.

Ask your parents to join in an event at school. Maybe they can't be official "room parents," but they might be able to go along on a field trip, help out with a project, or volunteer at the carnival.

TOP **TEN** WAYS *to Make Sure*
YOU GET **YELLED AT** BY YOUR PARENTS

10. Keep your room in a state of total chaos. Make sure it's disgusting beyond belief. How? Stuff your pajamas under your bed, wad your clean clothes in a heap on the bed, have wood shavings from your guinea pig/hamster cage all over your rug, throw a few items of clothing around for decoration, leave your Rollerblades and sports equipment smack dab in the middle of the floor for your parents to trip on in the dark, and above all, never, never, never make your bed or shut your closet doors.

9. Let your furry little pet run around the linen closet on the clean towels and sheets.

8. Surprise your parents on occasion by going somewhere totally different than where you said you were going to go. That way when they call to come and pick you up, they won't know where you are. Surprise! (They'll just love it.)

7. By all means, don't tell your parents when you have a big project due at school. You don't want them nosing around, asking a lot of questions, expecting you to be working on it, and junk like that.

6. Sneak off to the mall or a movie without telling your parents. This works especially well if they're not home and might not even find out you're gone. Of course, it's a bit of a sticky mess if they come home and you're not there . . . .

5. Make up a really stupid story rather than tell the truth. Sometimes you luck out and your parents fall for your tale. But you have to be careful with this one because most parents weren't born yesterday and they seem to know when you're making up a really ridiculous story.

4. Whine. Oh, yes. Whine, whine, and whine some more. That really irritating whine that drives your parents right up a wall. The kind that makes them consider moving your room out to the garage because they can't stand being around you for one more minute. That kind of whine. A definite must.

3. Argue with them each and every time they say no. Sure-fire results.

2. Disagree at every opportunity. If they say "Up," you say, "Down." If they say, "It happened this way," you jump in and say, "No, it happened that

way." If they say "It happened Tuesday," you be sure and correct them and say, "It happened Wednesday." Anything to say the opposite. Anything to disagree and make them look stupid and incompetent. They love it.

And the number one best way to get yelled at by your parents:

When all else fails, sulk. Oh, yes. Especially if they want you to go along somewhere with them. Act like you are doing them an enormous favor. Act like it's going to totally ruin your day and your social life to have to go along. Be obnoxious. Be impossible. Ruin everyone's afternoon. That will definitely do the trick. But then, consider yourself totally, completely, permanently sunk. Plan on spending the rest of your life in your room—with every single person in your family mad at you.

Chapter 7

"Hey, That's NOT FAIR!"

The world is full of wonderful, helpful, friendly people. But there are also people in this world who aren't very friendly. Some people will take advantage of you, try to make you feel bad about yourself, or try to hurt you in some way.

Dear Brave New Girl:

Sometimes I feel yucky about myself. I look at all the really cute girls on TV shows and movies and I feel so ugly in comparison to them. And I love to read all the teen magazines but I end up feeling so jealous and hopeless. I'll never be able to dress like that or have all that neat stuff in my room. Sometimes I spend so much time trying to get my hair right and look really great, and I still don't look like all the girls in the magazines. Then when I get to school, there are some kids (boys and girls) who are always teasing me. They call me fat and say I have pimples. And to top it all off, someone ripped off all my stuff from my locker—good stuff, too. Stuff I wanted. I think I know who did it, but I can't prove it. Yuck. What a day. Is there any help for me?

> SIGNED,
> IT'S JUST NOT FAIR

Dear It's Just Not Fair:

Wow, you've brought up lots of stuff here. It sounds like:

you feel picked on by others,

> you feel like you would be liked more if you looked more like the people on TV or in the magazines,

> > you're being teased at school.

It's really hard not to compare yourself to the movie and magazine models, isn't it? Imagine looking like that and having all those cool clothes, cars, boyfriends, and parties. Real life can be a lot tougher than a page out of a magazine, can't it? It's hard to realize and accept that we don't have bodies like models. And remember that all the cool clothes they wear in the pictures are being loaned to them for the photos or movie. Most real girls don't have that much money, clothing, or time to fuss about how they look.

As for being teased at school, could you talk to your homeroom teacher or a counselor? Sounds like things are pretty tough for you and it's important to remember that you don't have to handle your problems all alone. Talk to a grown-up who can help you figure out a plan that will work for you. You could:

Confront the student who took your things (perhaps with a teacher present) and at least let the person know how you feel.

Build a bridge of communication with those who tease you, saying "hello" without leaving yourself available for more teasing (or avoid these people until things cool down).

What can you do to stay safe and strong in a world that isn't always girl-friendly?

HERE ARE SOME TIPS TO KEEP IN MIND, THEN READ ON FOR MORE:

Be aware of the messages the media sends out about violence, girls, and women. TV shows, movies, and magazines often give messages that it's somehow okay to hurt girls and women. Or else they make girls and women feel bad about themselves, telling them they aren't good enough, thin enough, busy enough, or don't have the right clothes or hairstyle.

Tell an adult if anyone tries to harass you or scares you. You don't have to put up with being teased by mean kids or grown-ups.

Choose friends who treat you with respect and kindness.

Be clear about the rules your parents and school have that help keep you safe. Ask if you're not sure why a rule is there and try to understand how it keeps you safe and healthy.

MEDIA

Let's take a quick look at the media. What exactly is the media? It's things like TV, movies, videos, magazines, news programs, and newspapers. There is plenty about the media that is fun, funny, interesting, and entertaining. But, you have to be super-watchful about what else the "media" tells you about girls, women, and YOU.

Many people and organizations are working hard to make this world a brighter and better place for everyone. But some people and some companies just want to sell you something. They want you to believe what they say and buy their product so they will make money. How can you tell the difference? Who should you believe? Let's start by taking a look at some of the messages girls and women receive from the media (TV, radio, movies, magazines) as they go through their day.

THE REAL WORLD VS. TV *and the* Media

Have you ever noticed how much violence against girls and women there is on television and in the movies? It's amazing how often girls and women are mistreated in the media. Girls and women are slapped, stalked (followed), raped, terrorized, pushed, shoved, called names, frightened, hit, and even killed. Sometimes the whole show is about a girl or woman being attacked in some way and a boy or man rescuing her and solving the crime. It's to the point where it's hard to find a movie where at least one girl or woman is not being hurt.

Movies and TV shows also show girls being airheads or bubbleheads and acting stupid and silly. Girls are made to look dumb and whiny, or else like big mouths who are only interested in their hair, boys, and what to wear.

The "entertainment industry" is made up of all the people and companies who create the movies and television shows. They are not only trying to entertain you, they are trying to make as much money as possible from you. They have found that people enjoy watching violence, especially violence against girls and women. People are willing to pay a lot of money to see shows with a lot of violence.

Because these companies make tons of money selling these movies, they continue to make more of them. Lots more. They don't seem to care that people are getting the message from these movies that it's okay to hurt girls and women. After a while, it gets hard to even "see" or "hear" the violence against girls and women. People in the audience (all of us) have gotten so used to seeing girls and women mistreated that we doesn't realize when it's happening.

Consider the TV shows and movies you watch. As an experiment, list a few movies (in the theater or on video) you have seen in the past few months. Try to recall any examples you can think of when a girl or woman was treated badly. Think hard and you may be surprised at how many examples you can come up with.

Movie name:

Bad things happening to girls/women:

Movie name:

Bad things happening to girls/women:

Movie name:

Bad things happening to girls/women:

Take this book along with you each time you watch TV for the next few days. List the shows you are watching and how girls/women are treated.

List the times they are treated well:

Now list the times they are treated disrespectfully:

Be sure to include commercials. Maybe girls or women are not being mistreated, but what is the message being given to them? Are they being told they are too fat or that there is something wrong with their hair, clothes, or body that would be "fixed" if they bought the fancy product being shown? Are the girls or women acting like they don't know anything or have no brain in their head? Are their bodies being used to sell something totally different, like a car or beer?

Watch and listen carefully to the words used toward women. Are people talking to girls/women with respect, or do they speak to them sarcastically as if they were stupid?

How are they treated, especially by boys and men?

What is the topic of conversation? Is it about sex and their bodies?

Now make a statement about how girls and women were treated in each of the shows you watched. What kind of messages are these shows giving to the world?

TV show/commercial:

Girls and women are:

TV show/commercial:

Girls and women are:

TV show/commercial:

Girls and women are:

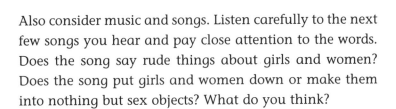

Also consider music and songs. Listen carefully to the next few songs you hear and pay close attention to the words. Does the song say rude things about girls and women? Does the song put girls and women down or make them into nothing but sex objects? What do you think?

ACTION PLAN!
What Do I Think?

After you have watched and kept track of a few TV shows and commercials, what do you think? How have you seen girls and women treated?

One of the best ways to fight this problem of girls/women being mistreated in the media is to let the companies know what you think!

If every girl who reads this book would write just one letter to the TV station or company sponsoring the show (the company advertising during the commercials), things might get better for girls and women everywhere.

Let the TV shows and movie companies know what YOU think about how girls and women are treated in the media. Let them hear your opinion. Be sure to state your age and sign your name. Let them know that product buyers (that's you) have strong opinions and care about how girls and women are treated.

If you write a letter, you will probably get a letter back because they care about what you think and whether you will buy what they are selling.

Here's How!

 **BRAVE LETTERS**

You may be embarrassed or a little scared to write a letter to a humongous television station. You're not alone! How do you work up your courage to write this letter? Here's some ideas and tips followed by info on where to send your gutsy letter.

Talk to yourself while looking in the mirror. Say what you really think about the TV show or movie. This is a way to practice expressing what you think and feel.

Next, jot a few of your cool ideas down on a piece of paper.

Tell yourself that you certainly have a right to your opinions. Give yourself the message that you are using your voice and words to make this world a better place and that it's important that you work hard to clean this world up for girls and women everywhere.

Practice writing down what you want to say. Your letter can be as long or as short as you'd like.

What Do I Say?

You may be wondering exactly how to write your letter. Here's a chance to think through a few ideas and a sample letter.

Ask your friends to write one with you.

Use a typewriter, a home computer, or just a plain old piece of paper—whatever you have on hand.

Remember, it doesn't have to be perfect. The main idea here is to express your opinion.

Take a look at the sample letter on the next page. Don't copy this one and send it; it's important that you make up your own. This is just to give you a few ideas to get you started.

Date

Dear XYZ Company:

My name is _____ and I'm eleven years old and in the sixth grade. I was watching the TV show "Name of Show" on Thursday night and I was very upset to see how badly the main female character, Joanna, was treated. It seemed like a few of the men felt they could harass her and make her feel uncomfortable by the way they looked at her and treated her. And then later in the show, a man tried to kidnap her and another man had to come and rescue her.

I think that women should be treated with more respect. I think your TV show made it look like it's okay to hurt women and I don't like it. I'm not going to watch your show again and I'm not ever going to buy any of the products your advertisers sell.

Sincerely,
Your name and signature
Your address

Now It's Your Turn

Use this space to write your first draft of a letter to a TV station, movie company, or product company. Tell them exactly what you think, then look over what you've written. Then write your real letter and send it off. Don't forget to include your name, age, and return address. Go for it!

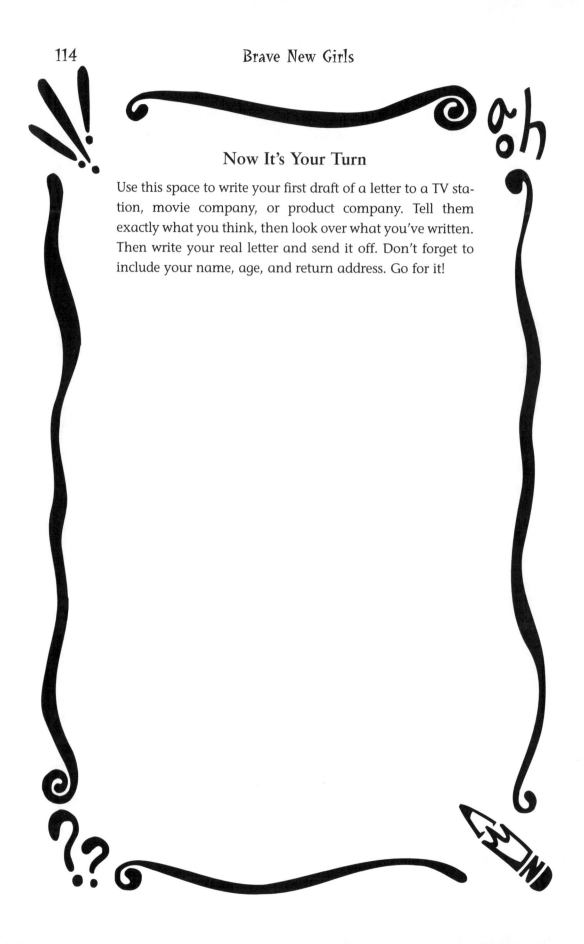

Write your letter today and make a difference in the world!

You may be wondering who to send the letter to and how to get the right address. If it's a TV show, you can write to the local TV station in your city. Even better, write to the big network headquarters (most are in New York City). Ask your parents which network the TV show is on. Here are the addresses of the TV networks:

ABC: 77 W. 66th St., New York, NY 10023

CBS: 51 W. 52nd St., New York, NY 10019

FOX: P.O. BOX 900, Beverly Hills, CA 90213

NBC: 30 Rockefeller Plaza, New York, NY 10112

PBS: 1320 Braddock Place, Alexandria, VA 22314

If it's a show on cable television, check the TV guide in your newspaper. All the addresses of the cable stations are usually listed in the big Sunday paper.

Movies

If it's a movie you saw in a theater, have your parents contact directory assistance on the telephone and get a phone number and/or address for the movie company. (Many libraries will give you this information, too.) The company that made the movie is always listed at the beginning and end of the movie. Most companies are located in New York or California.

PRODUCTS

It's easy to find out the name of the company that made a product that's being advertised. Just go to the store and look at the product. Somewhere on the side of the package is the name of the company and the address to write them.

STAND UP AND SPEAK OUT!

Can't Go to the Movies?

What if your parents won't even let you check out all the movies and stores that you friends get to go to? After all, you're probably thinking, you're certainly old enough to see these things for yourself. See what "Can't Go" has to say.

Dear Brave New Girl:

My parents don't let me go to see all the new movies. I feel so stupid and left out when my friends talk about the movie they saw last weekend and my parents say I can't go. It's the same for TV shows. I can't watch most of the shows my friends can, and they all talk about what they watched the next day. My parents say everything is too violent or grown up for me to watch, or that I'm too young. How can I convince them that I'm old enough to see the movies my friends see? And, another thing. They don't let me go to the mall alone with my friends, either. By the way, I'm eleven years old.

    Signed,
    Can't Go

Dear Can't Go:

I bet you wish you had different parents right about now! I mean, if your friends get to see R-rated movies and sexy sitcoms, and their parents drop them off at the mall for an afternoon of shopping, why shouldn't you be able to do the same thing, right?

Unfortunately, a lot of today's movies and even TV sitcoms are pretty trashy. They show scary, hateful things on the screen and make it look like violence is okay, that hurting and even killing other people is just business as usual. Now you're probably saying, "I know it's just a movie or TV. I know it's not real and I would never, ever do those things myself. So why can't I go?"

You're absolutely right—it is just a movie and it's not real. The problem is that it sends out messages that violence is okay. How? Just by showing the violence in the first place. Some people act out the violence they see in movies and on TV for real. If you put too much of that junk in your brain it starts to take hold, and pretty soon you feel fears and angry feelings that you wouldn't have felt if you hadn't watched that stuff.

As far as the mall shopping goes, my guess is that your parents trust you, but they don't trust everybody else. They know that although most people are friendly, some people can't be trusted and are pretty mean to kids. They want you to be safe and enjoy your shopping trip. With an adult along, mean people are not as likely to bother and hassle you. Maybe you could negotiate to go off with your friend for a period of time while your parents hang out in the same general area so you'd have a little more privacy. Remember, they trust you, but they don't trust people they don't know.

So take heart in the fact that you will grow up a lot healthier, less scared, and safer by holding off on going to garbage movies and putting yourself in unsafe shopping situations. Good luck!

MAGAZINES AND ADVERTISEMENTS

Have you noticed that most TV shows, movies, and magazines focus on girls being beautiful, thin, acting pretty stupid, and being put down? They make a big deal about how you look. You're supposed to be skinny and have super-cute clothes and every day is supposed to be a really great hair day. Magazines teach that the most important things in the world are how you look and how to get and keep a boyfriend.

You may like these things yourself, and that's just fine. There's nothing wrong with you for liking stuff. What's important is that your whole life shouldn't turn into a major fashion show for others. You need to find what's important and meaningful to you. Like what, you ask? Things like treating your body in a healthy way, being a really great friend who is kind, understanding, and easy to talk to, helping someone else with a problem they may be having (whether it's a friend with math homework or an older neighbor who can't mow her lawn anymore). You get the picture. It's hard to find a magazine that takes girls seriously and gets real about real girl issues.

New Moon Magazine is a shining star among girls' magazines. *New Moon* is written by girls and takes the dreams, ideas, and voices of girls very seriously. (Read all about these girls in the *New Moon* profile in Chapter 9.) You'll be impressed and excited about their ideas and energy. Way to go, *New Moon!*

You'll also want to check out *Teen Voices* magazine, which talks about very real issues for teens in a healthy way.

Don't hate me because I'm beautiful . . .

Sadly, there aren't many other magazines for girls who live real lives—lives that are more than just make-up, hair, and clothes. Of course, most girls want to look their best, but there are a bazillion more important things in life than how you look and dress.

Another problem is that the media gives girls the message that there is something wrong with them. How? By telling them (you) how to "fix" some imagined "flaw" (problem) about yourself. The media tells you:

That you need all kinds of extra products to make yourself look and smell right.

Your haircut, your face and your clothes are what really matter instead of what kind of a girl you are on the inside.

The "Right" Clothes

Of course, you want to be clean and fresh, with shiny hair, brushed teeth, and clean clothes. This is perfectly normal and good. And most girls want to feel like they "fit in." However, many girls don't feel good about themselves unless they have the "right" clothes that look exactly like what their friends are wearing. Clothing companies have cleverly printed the name of their company on the outside of clothes so now everybody knows whether you are wearing the "right" (meaning expensive) clothes.

Isn't it fun to have a new outfit to wear? Everyone enjoys fresh, new clothes. It's fun to express yourself through the clothes you choose. The problem comes in when you don't feel good unless you're wearing the "right" clothes or shoes.

All the advertisements you see and hear give you the message that if you buy and wear the "right" clothes, shoes, and hair products, you will fit in with everyone else and you will be happier. What a trap! If you think about it, you may realize how utterly ridiculous that is. The real you has nothing to do with what you're wearing or what products you have purchased at the store. The color of your lips or hair, the brand of jeans or shoes you have on, the shape of your body, or how much you weigh has absolutely nothing to do with what kind of a girl you are on the inside—for real.

Does Buying Something Equal Happiness?

Does buying stuff make you feel happy? Maybe for a while. But for how long, really? Think about the stuff you have purchased lately (or asked your parents to get for you).

Think about something new you've gotten in the past few weeks.

Item I bought or received:

How much did you want it at the time?

a little   *a lot*

1   2   3   4   5   6   7   8   9   10

How important to you is it now (at least 2 weeks later)?

a little   *a lot*

1   2   3   4   5   6   7   8   9   10

Would you have thought of it if you hadn't seen it on TV or known that a friend had one?

Yes   **No**

Besides the fact that you liked it, why did you buy the item?

When you bought the item, did you think it would make you feel happier?

a little   *a lot*

1   2   3   4   5   6   7   8   9   10

How long did the happy feeling last?

"GIRLCOTT" the Junk

Have you ever heard the term "boycott"? It means to avoid something you don't like or agree with. It means refusing to buy something or do something you don't think is right. How about if we create a new word—"girlcott"—to mean refusing to watch, buy, or go along with something that isn't friendly or respectful to girls? You could decide what magazines, TV shows, movies, or neat-looking stuff at the store you want to avoid because it doesn't make girls or women feel good about themselves. You can put your brain in gear and decide for yourself what's the right way to treat girls and what products you want to buy because they really have value.

You may feel funny and weird the first few times you do this. All your friends may want to try to get you to go along with them and you'll feel like you look really stupid for going your own way. It's okay to feel a little uncomfortable if you're doing what you think is right.

Some girls are natural leaders. They have an easy time saying, "This is what I want to do and this is what I think." Many other girls are natural followers. They prefer to "fit in" and go along with what everyone else seems to be doing. Whatever kind of person you are, sometimes it's important to stand up for what you think and believe is right for girls and women, and for you.

The media is trying to pull a fast one on you by convincing you that if you buy a particular product, you will be happier. But the happy feeling wears off pretty quickly, doesn't it? The media is also sending the message that it's okay to be violent, hurtful, and disrespectful to girls and women and that their bodies are up for grabs to be used for sex and to sell products.

Think for yourselves, girls. Don't get caught up in all the garbage and junk the media is trying to dump on you. Talk back! Write letters! Speak up! Don't spend your money on garbage!

What Do I Think?

I'm curious. What do you think about the ads you see in magazines and on TV? Especially ads for things like blue jeans—you know the ones, with girls wearing jeans and a short top while posing in sexy positions. Here's a questionnaire to help you decide what you think about all the ads.

Think of an ad that makes girls and boys look "sexy." Now answer:

1. Do I think this ad makes girls look bad?

    Yes   **No**

2. Does this ad make the girl look sexy?

    Yes   **No**

3. Do ads that make girls look sexy sell more products?

    Yes   **No**

4. Would I want to be a model for these kinds of ads?

    Yes   **No**

    WHY?

5. Should girls under 18 be allowed to pose in "sexy" positions for ads?

    Yes   **No**

6. Would I buy a product that uses advertising that I think is bad or wrong for girls' or women's image?

    Yes   **No**

7. Are girls or women being "used" when they pose for these types of ads?

    Yes   **No**

When Someone Doesn't Treat You Right Just Because You're a Girl

It's not only TV shows, movies, magazines, and commercials that don't treat girls right. Sometimes real people hurt girls. When people don't feel good about themselves, they sometimes hurt other people in order to make themselves feel more powerful and important. It doesn't make much sense, but it's true. Boys, other girls, and grown-ups can tease and harass you until you cry, scream, run, or feel really scared.

One afternoon on the school bus, Sarah was harassed by a bunch of boys who took her school bag and dumped it out, wouldn't let her sit down, and scared her out of her wits. She didn't know what to do, so she didn't do anything. When she got home she burst into tears and told her mom what happened. Her mom called the department of transportation (the school bus company) and reported what happened. The man on the phone said, "Well, the back of the bus is sort of the boys' turf, so maybe your daughter should just ride up in the front." Her mom was smart enough to say, "Excuse me, but my daughter should be able to ride anywhere on the school bus and be safe!" This mom found her voice and made a strong, clear statement.

Do you have any other ideas about how to handle this situation?

Being teased and harassed by a bunch of kids, grown-ups, or someone bigger is very scary. You usually feel too scared and startled to know what to do. It's a good idea to figure out ahead of time what you could do to protect yourself in case something happens. Sometimes there is nothing you can do, but it's always a good idea to try to keep yourself as safe and far away from danger as you can.

WHEN IS SOMEONE HARASSING ME?

Sometimes it's hard to know if someone is harassing you or just being a creep and bugging you. You are being harassed if:

You don't think it's funny and you are not enjoying "the joke."

You don't know the person or group of kids bothering you.

You ask them to stop and they don't.

You feel scared, creeped out, like running or crying, or you wish that someone would see what is happening and put a stop to it.

You don't feel safe.

You feel like the other person has more power and control than you do.

How Do I Stay Safe if Someone Harasses Me?

Here's a list of a few things you can do if someone harasses, teases, or tries to scare you:

Get away and get safe! Take any chance you have to leave the situation. You count and you're important.

Tell someone what happened to you. It may feel embarrassing, but it's important to report what happened, whether it's someone hassling you in the hallway at school or someone trying to grab your packages at the shopping mall.

Go ahead and yell at the creep who is bothering you. Don't be bashful—let the weirdo have an earful! (This will also alert others that you need help.) I know you may be embarrassed or afraid to do this, but your safety is of major importance here, so go ahead, be mad and yell.

Don't worry one second about hurting these bozos' feelings. Who cares if the person doesn't like what you're doing? People who harass girls don't deserve to be treated politely.

Report anyone who looks suspicious. For instance, let the police handle the weird-looking guy who is watching girls get on and off the school bus. Don't brush these situations off. Tell your parents, your teacher, and the police.

> **Remember that it's against the law to harm, hurt, hit, abuse, stalk, or terrorize girls!**

Melody is Asian-born and adopted into an American family. Her parents were white and she attended a school with mainly white kids. She hated it when kids called out "Chinese Eyes" as she walked down the hall. Melody was pretty outspoken, though, and tended to stop cold, turn and look at the kids with the big mouths and announce, "I'm not Chinese, I'm Korean!" Not that there's anything wrong with being Chinese, but rather than letting ignorance slide, Melody took every opportunity to educate others and shed light on cultural differences. She was proud of being Korean and let the world know it!

WHAT ELSE CAN MELODY DO?

Melody loved attending Korean Culture Camp in the summer. There she learned about her native country and how to be a foreign-adopted kid in a white family.

Melody and her mom suggested a Culture Day once a month at school. Someone could present information about a different country each month during school assembly. The presentation could include costumes, a native song, or interesting information about the country.

Melody also talked to her teacher, who felt it was important to discuss racial differences in a class meeting. Eventually these discussions were turned into a brochure, which was printed in the computer lab and given out to each student in the school. The brochure included information on how to handle racial harassment, important facts about different cultures, and tips on how to build bridges of communication instead of walls of anger and ignorance.

Way to go, Melody!

HURTFUL RELATIONSHIPS

You might be surprised to learn that girls and women are hurt most often by people they know. Even your own girlfriends can be mean to the point of being cruel.

AMY WAS TEASED BY HER FAMILY SO MUCH FOR BEING "FAT" THAT SHE DIETED UNTIL SHE LOST SO MUCH WEIGHT SHE HAD TO GO TO THE HOSPITAL.

Or there's Maggie, whose brother tried to kiss her and touch her when her parents weren't home.

Or Allison, who hated going to school because the girls in her class snickered and turned away from her every time she walked by.

Lanie was only fifteen years old, but already her boyfriend had hit her. He would tease her, saying, "You'd better just stay with me. You're so fat and ugly, who else would want you for a girlfriend?" Lanie started to believe him after a while. After all, no other guys ever called her.

Has This Happened to You?

There are so many sad stories of girls being hurt and mistreated by people they know. What can you do if this is happening to you, or you see it happening to someone else?

You don't have to handle this alone. I know it's hard and maybe even embarrassing to tell your parents, but it can be really helpful to talk it over with them, or a teacher, or school counselor. Your friends are great, but you need a grown-up to help you with this one. Sometimes parents don't want to believe this bad thing is happening to you. If your mom and dad don't believe you, tell an adult at school.

End any friendship with someone who hurts you physically! Someone who hurts you is not a real friend and you deserve to be treated with respect. You do not deserve to be hit, no matter what you did to the other person.

Write a letter to the newspaper telling your concerns about how people mistreat girls.

If you know the person who is bothering you, tell the person exactly how you feel about the way he or she treated you. Don't soften the words—say it like it is!

If a friend continues to treat you wrong and you've tried to talk it out but the relationship stays bad for you, you have every right to leave and not be friends anymore. It sounds drastic, but it's okay to set some ground rules and stick to them.

Girls can end up putting up with a lot of junk in relationships with their family and friends. We all struggle with relationships—it's not always smooth sailing. You might want to go back over the section on conflict resolution in Chapter 3. Learning how to stay out of fights and learning to put an end to them when they happen is important, but more important than anything is understanding that you do not have to put up with being treated in a lousy manner. You are a very good person and no one has the right to mistreat you. Everyone has fights and yells at each other from time to time. But no one has the right to hit you or make you feel lower than a crumb on the floor. If anyone tries to make you feel that way, tell them to take a long, one-way hike!

Gina was mad and scared. She didn't like Kimberly one bit, and she just tried to stay away from her. The problem? Kimberly had a bunch of friends who always hung out with her. They traveled down the halls at school in a pack. Tuesday afternoon, Kimberly decided to bug Gina, calling her really gross names, trying to drive her crazy. Then Kimberly shoved her, and Gina hit Kimberly back. Well, guess who just happened to be walking down the hall just then? Yup, you got it, the principal, Mr. Davanni. Gina and Kimberly both got detention. Gina was mad, since SHE didn't start it. What was she supposed to do—just stand there and get hit? And she was scared because Kimberly always traveled with her pack of pals, who continued to whisper nasty threats to Gina every time she walked by. Now what?

Gina and Kimberly had to meet with the school counselor to air their differences and tell their side of the story. They also used this meeting to talk about things like:

how to avoid messes like this in the future.

how else they could have handled the situation.

how the two girls could be at least polite to each other
instead of driving each other crazy.

They decided:

I don't have to get pulled into the let's-fight attitude.

I can ask the counselor for tips or help in dealing with the other girl.

I can take responsibility for my own decisions and behavior and not blame anyone else.

I can go to any classroom and ask for help if it looks like there's trouble ahead.

RUMOR *City*

Maria is in the fifth grade. She is smart and fun to be with and lots of kids like to be with her. Even so, someone in one of the other fifth-grade classes started a nasty, false rumor about her, and pretty soon all the fifth-grade classes were giggling and whispering about what Maria was "supposed" to have done. Maria was embarrassed and hurt by the totally false rumor. It didn't take long for her teacher, Ms. Lopez, to hear about it and talk to Maria about what on earth was going on. Maria was close to tears and angry too as she explained the scoop to Ms. Lopez. Maria decided to be really gutsy and face this head on. She decided to go to each of the fifth-grade classes and tell them exactly how she felt about being talked about behind her back and having this untrue rumor spread. The kids realized how hurtful they had been and many came up to Maria to apologize for their rude behavior. Maria felt a whole lot better and was able to concentrate again on school and not on how awful she felt. A brave and gutsy response by Maria solved the problem.

WORD FIND

SPEAK OUT	COMMUNICATE
SAFE	TELL
TV	MOVIE
ADS	MAGAZINE
HARASS	GIRLCOTT
RUMOR	MEDIA

```
A  I  D  E  M  J  K  N  P  X  S
D  M  S  G  I  R  L  C  O  T  T
S  O  X  A  S  S  S  A  R  A  H
C  V  F  X  F  T  E  L  L  V  T
R  O  M  U  R  E  I  V  O  M  Z
T  U  O  K  A  E  P  S  L  G  F
E  T  A  C  I  N  U  M  M  O  C
Y  U  E  N  I  Z  A  G  A  M  Q
W  S  X  P  H  V  M  T  I  Z  O
```

Celebrate

YOU!

Chapter 8

MY *Own* MONEY

What's It All About?

It's important to understand how money fits into your life and to begin thinking about how to earn and handle your own cash. Besides, someday you're going to need to earn enough to support yourself, so let's start thinking right now about how you can become smart and strong about money!

The Tale of the Disappearing Allowance

Dear Brave New Girl:

Help! I'm always broke. I get an allowance (although it's not as much as my friends get) and I try to hang on to my money, but it just disappears. My parents get mad at me for always asking for more money; they say I should keep track of my allowance better. I want to spend my money on so many different things, but it's gone by the end of the week. What can I do?

SIGNED,

POOR ME

Dear Poor Me:

Good news! This problem can be fixed. You are not doomed to a life of an empty allowance jar. You don't have to win a million dollars to be happy, but being broke is a serious bummer. As you've already discovered, a lot of fun things in life cost money and you want to have some of your own. Just a little planning ahead will help you have enough money to buy some of your favorite things. Here are some quick ideas to start you thinking, then be sure you read this whole chapter and pick out a few of the ideas that you think might work for you.

Keep the money you earn (from babysitting, mowing lawns, washing cars, or whatever you do) in a separate jar. At the end of the month, take maybe the first ten dollars off the top for yourself, then split the rest of the amount between yourself and your savings account. It's a quick way to save, and helps you start out each month with a bundle of cash.

Keep a money notebook (huge hint: Learn all about money notebooks beginning on page 138!), which shows the cash you bring in and the cash you spend each day or week. At least you'll know where it all went!

Have a special page in your money notebook to list all the things you're dreaming about buying. Look in the newspaper and check things out at the store to find out exactly how much money they cost. Put the cost down in your money notebook wish list. When you're tempted to blow a few bucks on something, remember your "wish list" and decide, "Do I really want this item, or do I want to keep saving up for what's on my wish list?"

These are just a few ideas to get you started. Read on for more!

MONEY TALK

Be strong and smart. Earn your own money by doing something you love to do.

Money is seriously cool stuff and it's really fun to have. You can learn to make as much as you want and use it in a positive way. Sound great? It is! As a Brave New Girl you will need to know how to earn, spend, and save money for the rest of your life. Forget waiting around for someone else to hand you the cash—you will be in charge of earning your money and supporting yourself as a woman (and possibly a mother with kids of your own to support). You might be thinking, "I'll probably get married someday and my husband is going to go to work and earn all the money I need." Not! Neither Prince Charming nor your parents are going to want to hand over the cash to keep you going. It's true that you may get married, but you can't expect your husband to take care of you or make enough money to support everyone. It's not a good idea to wait around and hope that someone else gives you money.

Money is definitely fun but it's also a big responsibility. You don't want to run out of cash as a grown-up. It's a real drag when there isn't enough to go around or when there's nothing left after the bills get paid. Remember, women have to work to support themselves and their families and so it only makes sense that girls and women learn everything they can about how money works.

Money doesn't have to be a big secret. You can talk about money just as easily as you talk about your homework or the softball game you won in gym. I know, I know, you can't stand the girls at school who act like they're so rich they can just buy everything they want. But, when you think about it, there are a lot of things in life that are simply wonderful and absolutely free. And these things are more important than money. Things such as:

Friends   *a healthy body*   **YOUR TIME**

hugs   **the air you breathe**   LAUGHTER

happiness   YOUR PET   *even your little brother*

a sunny day

Now, it's your turn to think of a few things to add to this list of other things you love that don't cost any money:

It's exciting to realize how much of what we have is free!

Of course, most things in life do cost money—things like where you live, your car, food, your clothes, your vacations, and all the things you want to buy, like CDs, movies, and cool earrings. Later, you'll even need to pay for things like haircuts and doctor visits. Plus, the older you get, the more things you'll want—and they will all cost money.

How Can I GET Some of my OWN CASH?

Not every job you do is going to bring you money as a reward. Everyone has some rather yucky, "thankless" tasks to do around the house. Your parents have to do the grocery shopping and errand running. Some jobs just have to be done (like picking up your clothes, feeding the guinea pig, and doing your homework), and the reward is simply a sense of order, accomplishment, and comfort. But there are ways you can earn some money for yourself. Here are some ideas for getting yourself some cash.

You could ask your parents for an allowance; maybe $2.00 a month for every year old you are. (For example, a ten-year-old would get $20.00 each month.) You may have to do some jobs around the house to earn it.

Find jobs in your neighborhood, such as babysitting, lawn mowing, car washing, or cat/dog/hamster feeding for vacationing neighbors.

Make up a flyer and drop it off at each house on your block offering to do any chores that you would feel capable of finishing.

Save some of your cash every single month so that you have a "nest-egg" of my own.

Have a "job jar" with little pieces of paper listing jobs that your parents (and sisters and brothers) will pay you to do. (My youngest daughter, a born-to-be-messy kid, sometimes pays her older sister, an orderly pack-rat, to help her clean up her room because once it's a complete disaster she doesn't like to do it all herself.) Make sure to have them put the amount they'll pay on the slip of paper so everyone knows ahead of time. It saves time and energy—there's no haggling over the price after the job's already been done.

You could team up with other family members or friends to do a major house project. The "pay" includes the fun of working together, getting silly, and finishing the project by ordering pizza with all your favorite toppings. You could even polish off more than one major project if you all work together. You could wash the car (inside and out), wash the windows, clean out the garage, clean out all the bedroom closets, or collect stuff you don't want anymore to donate to the organization of your choice.

You could find out if there is a new mom in your neighborhood. You might offer your services as a "mother's helper." Even though it's not as much pay as real babysitting, you could play with the baby while she gets her own tasks done. Also, you can help her with any other tasks she has to do around the house. You both win. She gets a ton of stuff done and you get some cash.

Money Power Checklist

Here's a chance to rate yourself on how much control you have over your money. Circle "Yes" or "No" (give yourself 5 points for every "Yes") or circle the number which best describes you and your situation. On a scale of 1 to 10 (with 1 = very little or almost never and 10 = a lot or all the time), answer these questions about yourself:

1. I get an allowance:

1   2   3   4   5   6   7   8   9   10

2. I keep track of my allowance money:

1   2   3   4   5   6   7   8   9   10

3. I keep track of my money in a special notebook:

1   2   3   4   5   6   7   8   9   10

4. I know how to balance and keep track of my savings account register:

1   2   3   4   5   6   7   8   9   10

5. I have earned some of my own money in the past year:

1   2   3   4   5   6   7   8   9   10

6. I talk with my parents about money:

1   2   3   4   5   6   7   8   9   10

7. I think about ways I can earn money now:

1   2   3   4   5   6   7   8   9   10

8. I think and plan about how to earn money when I'm a grown woman:

1   2   3   4   5   6   7   8   9   10

9. I have ideas about what kind of business I would like to start:

1   2   3   4   5   6   7   8   9   10

10. I make good choices about how I spend my money:

1   2   3   4   5   6   7   8   9   10

11. I have a savings account:

     Yes   No

12. I have my own checking account:

     Yes   No

13. I know how to balance a checking account:

     Yes   No

14. I think I will have to earn my own money as a grown woman:

     Yes   No

15. I think no one else will just support me and give me money when I am an adult:

     Yes   No

CHECK OUT WHERE YOU STAND

95–125: Go girl! You are taking responsibility for your money and for planning ahead. Keep going and you will be strong, successful, and totally in charge of your cash.

70–94: You're getting the idea. Now try to learn more about how to handle your money by keeping track of it, making good choices about what you buy, and by thinking up ways to earn more money.

45–69: Hey, you're trying, right? You just need to learn more about how money works. Ask your parents and friends about how they handle their money and if they have any good ideas for you.

10–44: Oops. The time has come for you to check out the money scene. Get some cash in your life and learn how to manage it. Have a serious talk with your parents, read this chapter, and go for it! Get yourself some money, girl!

Here's Katie

Katie wanted a guinea pig so much that she could hardly stand it. She asked her parents, but they said no. She was so disappointed and mad. All her good friends had pets and her science class had everything from turtles to mice. And she didn't have anything. Then Katie got a pretty clever idea. She wondered if her parents would be willing to say yes if she helped pay for the little furball herself. She sat down with her allowance jar and money book and figured she had a grand total of $19.73. (Well, it was a start.) Then she talked her idea over with her parents. Instead of whining and begging, she was able to talk to them about a great idea. She also did her homework to find out how much everything would cost: the cage, water bottle, bedding, food, exercise wheel, cage liners, and the pig itself (!). She learned that the grand total came to $117.84. She had only $19.73 to start. Now what? Katie thought about it for a while and decided to ask her parents if they would split the cost with her, and guess what? They said yes! Katie was jumping up and down with excitement. Then it occurred to her that she had to come up with $58.92. Her heart sank. Where on earth would she get that much money? It would take her a million years to save that much allowance money. Katie nearly cried until she had another great idea. Earn the money! "All right," she thought, "I can do this!" So, Katie made a plan of all the jobs she could do to earn money and set about doing a few each day. Soon, she and her parents were on the way to the pet store to purchase Fluffball, the newest member of the family. Katie figured out how to get something she really wanted by using her imagination, hard work, and determination. Go, Katie!

HERE'S WHAT I THINK

Here's your chance to put your brain in gear and think about money. Write down your own answers to the questions on the next page and don't worry about what anybody else thinks. What's important is to figure out what *you* think about money. Be honest. Be yourself. Tell the world what you think!

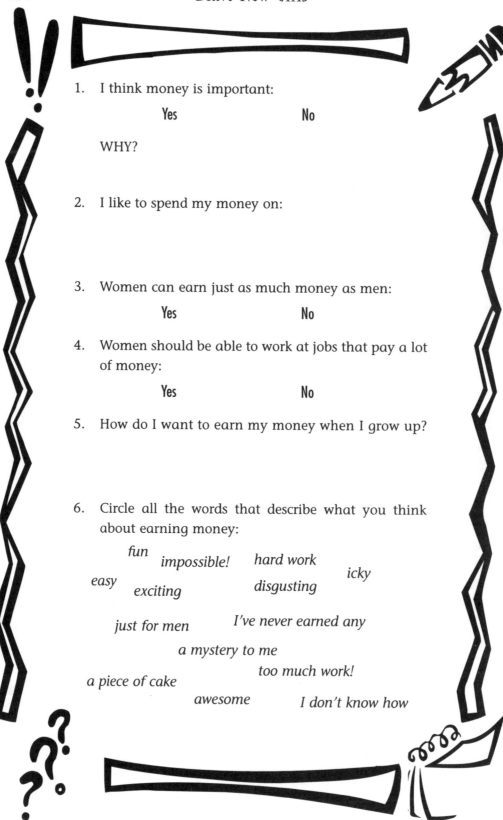

1. I think money is important:

            Yes   No

   WHY?

2. I like to spend my money on:

3. Women can earn just as much money as men:

            Yes   No

4. Women should be able to work at jobs that pay a lot of money:

            Yes   No

5. How do I want to earn my money when I grow up?

6. Circle all the words that describe what you think about earning money:

   fun

   impossible!   *hard work*

   easy   *exciting*   *disgusting*   *icky*

   just for men   *I've never earned any*

   a mystery to me

   a piece of cake   *too much work!*

   awesome   *I don't know how*

7. I could earn my own money now by:

8. Let's say I'm all grown up and maybe I'm even mar-
    ried and have two kids. Should I have to earn any
    money to help support the family?

                    Yes   No

    WHY?

9. Who is going to pay my bills when I grow up—bills
    like my rent or mortgage payment, my car, my food,
    my clothes, my fun money?

10. Why do you think it is that so many women seem to
    earn less money than men do?

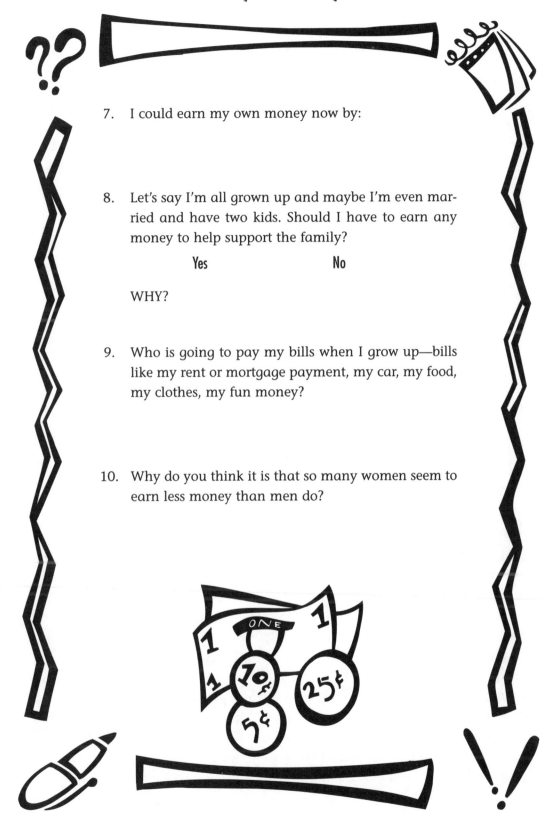

Magical **Thinking**

Too many girls and women get lost in "magical thinking" where they hope and plan on someone else paying for their life. Not! You must never think that when you are a grown-up woman, someone else is going to pay for your car, clothes, or anything else! You must plan on earning your own money to pay your bills, support yourself (and maybe your kids), and buy some of the goodies that you want.

When you are a girl, you can expect your parents to pay for most of what you need and want. But once you're grown up, you need to know how to bring the money in yourself. So, let's get started while you're still a growing girl, full of energy and great ideas and not worried about paying bills. If you start now, you won't have to worry about money and bills when you're a grown-up because you'll already know how to handle money.

Where does all my money go?

Money Notebooks

Hey girls, get yourself a special money notebook to keep track of your money! Here's how it works.

Amy decided she wanted to start keeping track of her money. She wanted to know when she had enough to buy that sweatshirt she wanted. Besides, she was tired of wondering where her money kept going. How could she start the week with $20.00 and then by the end of the weekend find only a few measly pennies and dimes in her allowance jar? She couldn't even remember what she bought! I mean, where did it all go? So, Amy scraped together a little cash and asked her parents to take her along when they went to run errands. She bought a nifty little notebook that looked like a real "money book" and had special lines and columns in it to help keep track of the amount she got and the amount she spent. (She saw a lot of regular spiral notebooks, too, that she could have used. All she would have had to do was draw lines from top to bottom and it would look the same.) Here is an idea of what Amy's money notebook looked like. She used two pages each month, one page for cash and one for savings.

MONEY NOTEBOOK FOR CASH

Month:	September		Year:	1998	
Date	Item	Out	In	Balance
9-1-98	allowance		$20.00	$20.00
9-3-98	babysitting (half of $11.00)		$5.50	$25.50
9-7-98	pair of earrings	$3.50		$22.00
9-10-98	cleaned garage for neighbor		$4.00	$26.00
9-15-98	hair stuff	$5.00		$21.00
9-15-98	ice cream cone	$1.25		$19.75
9-22-98	Cool CD	$14.00		$5.75
9-28-98	babysitting (half of $6.00)		$3.00	$8.75
9-30-98	movie and candy	$7.00		$1.75

At least Amy now knows what happened to her $20.00 allowance and all her earned money. But Amy has more money, too. She's got her savings jar money (she keeps the record for that on a different page in her notebook). Each week she does work around the house and her parents pay her for it, and she puts that money in her savings account jar. At the end of the month, she takes the first $10.00 for herself and divides the rest of it in half. She puts half in her savings account and half in her allowance jar to keep for herself. Amy's feeling pretty rich these days.

Savings Accounts

Dear Brave New Girl:

Every time I get some money for my birthday or a holiday, my parents make me put most of it into my savings account at the bank. What a drag! There's so many things I want to buy, but all my money just gets stashed away at some bank. It's not fair! It's my money, so shouldn't I be able to do whatever I want with it?

SIGNED,

STUCK IN THE BANK

Dear Stuck In the Bank:

Yes indeed, it is your money! But you want to be smart about how you use it. How about splitting the money? Have a talk with your parents and offer to split it between your savings account and your fun money jar. Perhaps you could split it right in half, or in thirds (one third for you to spend and two thirds in the bank). This way you will be able to still have some fun while fattening up your piggy bank.

Why **SAVE** All That Good Money
When I Could **SPEND** it & Have FUN?

Good question. An interesting thing about savings accounts is that you can get really cool stuff with the money you save. Think about it.

The more money you put into your savings account, the more it will grow and get fatter and fatter and fatter. I know it seems like an eternity to wait so long, but when you're eighteen or older, you will be thrilled to realize you have a huge "nest egg" of saved money to help pay for college, buy a car or a house, take a fabulous trip, or just keep saving it to see how much you can get. It's fun and adventurous to prepare for the kind of future you want to have!

You can also ask your parents to help you fill your savings account. Check out these wild numbers.

Let's say you and your parents save **$25** a month at **10%** interest, starting when you are eight years old. If you stop adding to the money when you are eighteen and just leave it in savings earning 10% until you are sixty-five years old (!) and ready to retire, you would have **$397,162.98!** *That's almost half a million dollars!*

Even better is if you and your parents save **$100** a month at **10%** interest from the time you are eight years old until you turn eighteen. If you keep the money in savings at 10%, guess how much you would have when you turn sixty-five? Are you ready? You would have **$1,588,651.03!** *That, dear girl, is over one and a half million dollars!*

SO, DOES SAVING MONEY SEEM LIKE A BETTER IDEA NOW?

What's a Good Way to Handle my Allowance?

Do you get an allowance? It doesn't really matter how often you get it or how much you get. You can put this cash to good use and learn a lot about how to handle your money. Every family does allowance differently, and that's okay. Some girls have to earn their allowance and others are just given the money.

One way to handle your allowance is to divide it into three different jars.

1. **One jar is for your "allowance," or spending money.** Whenever this jar gets a certain amount of money in it, deposit it into your checking account for safe keeping.

2. **A second jar is for savings**—the money you want to stuff into your savings account at the bank.

3. **A third jar is for "sharing."** Put some of your allowance money aside to help others. Once a year you can write a check to the group of your choice that needs extra money—you might choose a homeless shelter, food shelf, church, or a group working to save the environment—whatever or whoever touches your heart. Send a letter along with your check and you'll probably get a hearty "thank you" letter back from them.

Rich & FAMOUS?

Many girls dream of being rich and famous. It's okay to dream, but actually most girls and women won't be rich and/or famous. They'll live interesting lives, but they'll have to pay attention to "earning a living." Working to earn a living certainly does not have to be boring. You can earn your money doing something you really enjoy—something you are really good at. Different careers and jobs pay different amounts of money. Think about how much money you want to earn. Check out different types of jobs and find out how much women doing that job earn every month.

Sarah was surprised at how much money she had made babysitting over the summer. She had been saving it in a jar and when she counted it up, it came to a whopping $90.00. She ran up the stairs to tell her parents how rich she was, then started daydreaming about what to do with all her money. She really wanted a new CD player, but she also wanted to take skiing lessons this winter and her parents said she'd have to help pay for them. Then there was this book club she wanted to join and the best jeans and sweatshirt ever that she saw at the mall last Saturday. She knew without adding it up that everything she wanted was going to come to a lot more than $90.00. Now what? Suddenly, instead of feeling hyper-excited, she felt bummed out.

What can Sarah do?

Put her "rewards" in the order of how important they are to her. This is called "prioritizing." Even though she can't have everything she wants right now, maybe she can get them over the next few months.

Sarah can think about ways to earn more money.

Sarah can "brainstorm" with her friends and parents about what to do. Brainstorming is sitting around and talking with others to come up with a bunch of good ideas instead of feeling stuck with just one idea.

Sarah can put a part of the money toward her top two favorite rewards and keep adding to each until she can go ahead and get one.

ENTREPRENEURIAL GIRLS

What in the world is "entrepreneurial"? Good question. Being entrepreneurial is to strike out on your own and own your own business—you are in charge, the Head Banana, the Big Cheese. The great thing about owning your own business and being in charge is that no one can fire you—no one can make you lose your job. Besides that, you get to do the things you like to do and are really good at. Sure, even if you're in charge you have to do some boring things, but at least it's your own business—it's your store, your company, your ideas.

Of course, not every girl (soon to be woman) wants to own and run her own business. That's perfectly okay. The thing to think about is always having at least some small part of your work life run just by you, even if it's just some small "on-the-side" activity. That way you "own" a little more of your time, and you aren't dependent on someone else to like you and pay you to work for them. As a matter of fact, you can run a small business for yourself right now!

Setting up Shop

Imagine, girls. You can begin now—today—to own your own business. It can be a big idea with big-time results, or just a tiny, small-time idea. The size of the idea doesn't matter. What matters is that it's important to you and you put your heart, time, and energy into it. In other words, you put your dream or idea into action. Remember, you are your business!

You can turn almost any idea into a business. Is there something you would like to try making or a service you think you can provide? Maybe you enjoy designing bead necklaces or are great at mowing lawns. Perhaps you have completed a babysitting class or do a fabulous job washing cars. The sky's the limit—you can set up a small business doing anything your mind can dream up and your energy can make happen.

Ideas for ways you can earn money right now:

DELIVER NEWSPAPERS   *Babysit*

MOW LAWNS   **Rake leaves**

Water the garden   RUN ERRANDS FOR
twice a week   ELDERLY NEIGHBORS

The future seems like an awfully long way off, doesn't it? In a way, it is. Yet now is the perfect time to try out one of your ideas for earning money. You can give it a whirl without losing any money or having to worry about paying your own rent or buying groceries. You can use this time to experiment and see if your creative ideas bring you any cash. One summer, my kids and another girl in the neighborhood decided to make mini-pillows to sell. They gathered pieces of colorful fabric, stuffed them with cotton, and sewed them together. They carried the fabric samples around in a notebook and let customers choose their own combinations. They didn't get fabulously rich, but they did have fun, earned some cash, and most important, they tried out an idea.

Go ahead and choose a business idea. It can be anything that someone is willing to pay you to do. Write a couple of your ideas here:

1.

2.

3.

Now think about whether there is anything you will need to put your idea into action, like a lawn mower, information flyers, a calendar (to schedule babysitting, petsitting, etc.), or a computer for a newsletter.

What do I need?

Where can I get the supplies I need?

Here's an important question: How much will you charge for your service or product? It can be hard for many girls to look an adult in the eye and state her "fee" or what she charges for her work. Many girls feel embarrassed and just look at the floor, shrug their shoulders and say, "Whatever. It doesn't matter." You don't need to be embarrassed to ask for money for a job well done! Here are some tips to help you talk about how much money you will charge for your time.

Ask around. Find out what your friends charge and what the "going rate" is in your neighborhood.

Decide ahead of time on your price.

Run the amount you plan to charge past your parents and get feedback from them.

Be really brave and look the person in the eye when you state your price.

If you have more than one service or product to offer, make a written list on a bright-colored piece of paper, listing your services and prices for all the world to see. Print up at least a dozen of these "price lists" so you have a few handy for new customers.

Decide if you are willing to "negotiate" or discuss different prices. Or are you firm on your price and unwilling to change? If you do negotiate, be sure you don't just go along with the price an adult suggests (especially if it's lower than what you want!).

Increase your prices at the end of each year. This is called a "cost of living increase." Everything costs more each year, including your service or product.

What Should I Do if Someone Doesn't Pay Me?

Sometimes even the best people "forget" to pay a bill. But sometimes people choose to forget to pay, especially if they're dealing with a kid. This isn't fair, but it's true. Here are some ideas about how to handle people who are late in paying or don't pay at all.

Sometimes people will tell you (after you have done the babysitting or lawn mowing) that they don't have the right change or enough cash, and can they bring the money over later or pay you next time? In this case you're rather stuck, but only the first time they do this to you. If they don't bring the money within one day, call them and politely request the amount they owe you. If they still don't pay, call again. If they won't pay within three days, you may want to have your parents give them a call.

If someone has done this to you one time, be sure and remind them before you work for them again that you need to be paid at the end of the job, today. When you agree to do the job (probably over the phone) is the best time to say, "I would appreciate being paid as soon as the job is done."

If someone sticks it to you twice, don't work for them again and tell them why. "I'm sorry; I can't do that job for you because I haven't been paid for the last two times."

If your parents are doing this to you, show them this book and talk to them about how to solve the problem in the future.

Request cash rather than a check. It's hard for kids to get to the bank to cash checks.

What if Someone Goofs up the Math?

Roxanne babysat three kids from 1:30 to 6:30 P.M. on Saturday. She charged $5.00 an hour. When the Wilsons got home, Mrs. Wilson smiled, said thanks, and gave Roxanne $20.00. Oops. Roxanne thought, "Wait a second. 1:30 to 6:30 is five hours, not four. The Wilsons owe me $25.00, not just $20.00."

What should Roxanne do?
a. Smile sweetly, say, "Thank you," and leave.

b. Wait until next time, then remind Mrs. Wilson that she still owes her $5.00 from last time.

c. Politely, but clearly, say, "Mrs. Wilson, I babysat for five hours. That will be $25.00."

IF YOU ANSWERED:
a. Not! Roxanne deserves every penny she earned.

b. Nope. No need to wait for her money. Besides, Mrs. Wilson won't remember how many hours she was there.

c. Go, Roxanne!

Be clear about how much you charge and be sure to collect everything that is owed you. Be polite, but firm. You work hard and deserve to be treated fairly!

Some DOS and DON'TS when Starting your Business

DO

Dress for the job. You don't want to wear your fabulous new jeans if you're going to be doing lawn and garden work. Nor do you want to look like you just got out of bed if you're going to be introducing yourself to new people. Be sure you're squeaky clean. Who wants a smelly babysitter? No one will hire you or call you back if you look like you just crawled out of the dirty laundry pile.

DON'T

Call at the last possible second and tell them you can't come or can't deliver your product.

DO

ALWAYS BE ON TIME. MAKE SURE YOU ALLOW ENOUGH TIME TO ACTUALLY GET WHERE YOU'RE GOING. CALL IMMEDIATELY IF YOU THINK YOU'RE GOING TO BE LATE.

DO

Be clear about the amount you charge and be certain to collect everything that is owed you.

DON'T

Forget to show up or just not bother to call if you can't come. Talk about rude!

Dear Brave New Girl:

Help! My parents make me babysit my dumb little sister and brother whenever they go shopping or to the movies. It's hard work, too. I have to feed them, keep them from fighting, and make sure they don't burn down the house. The problem is that my parents never pay me for it and I miss doing fun stuff with my friends. Mom and Dad just say, "You can help out around here, and you can do that by babysitting." They're my parents; what can I do?

SIGNED,

STUCK BABYSITTING

Dear Stuck Babysitting:

Yours is an important and common problem for many girls. You might consider negotiating with your parents.

Ask them to give you advance notice that they would like you to babysit.

Talk with them about how many hours they want you to babysit for free. They may feel that this is doing your part to help the family (like helping with the dishes, raking the lawn, or sorting the laundry). Make agreements about how often babysitting will be expected of you. Mark it down on the calendar so everyone is clear.

Then, offer to "trade" with them. Offer to babysit in exchange for something you want, such as having a friend sleep over, extra TV time, or a ride to a friend's house.

Have a willing attitude. Remember that you have responsibilities around the house, but also remind your parents that after a certain amount of time you would like to "trade" babysitting time for fun time for you!

the facts

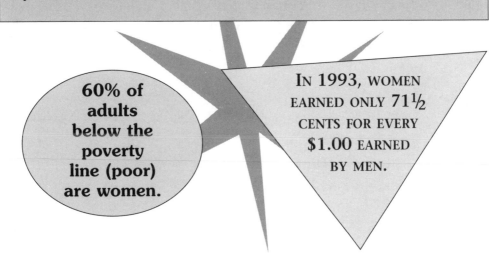

Society still tells girls they have a choice as to whether or not they will work for pay. Yet women are nine times as likely as men to be single parents and support their kids by themselves.

60% of adults below the poverty line (poor) are women.

IN 1993, WOMEN EARNED ONLY 71½ CENTS FOR EVERY $1.00 EARNED BY MEN.

Expect the Best From a Girl. That's What You'll Get. Women's College Coalition.

U.S. Census Bureau.

Minnesota Women's Economic Action Plan, The Minnesota Women's Consortium, 1991-92.

Planning for Success

Success is anything you want it to be. Success can be earning lots of money, being really happy, loving your work, raising a family, or having good friends. You can decide for yourself what you think is success for you. Nobody else gets to tell you what's successful and right for you.

You have to think about success ahead of time. Success doesn't just happen overnight or by magic. You have to plan for success. It's like playing in a piano recital or being in a swimming tournament. You can't just sit down at the piano or jump into the pool without ever practicing and expect to win.

THE PERFECT WORK DAY FOR ME

Begin today to dream about what the perfect day on the job will be for you. Play around with ideas about what you would like a for-real work day to look and feel like. Do you have some ideas about what kinds of work you might like to do? List a few things you might like to do to earn a living someday:

Do you see yourself working for someone else or owning your own business?

Let's work on planning a fantasy work day. You get to be the boss of how your day looks—you're in charge!

READY?

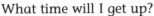

What time will I get up?

Where will I go to do my work? An office? An office in my home? A big company?

What kind of clothes will I wear to work? A uniform? Jeans? A business suit?

What kinds of people will I work with? Kids? Other grown-ups? Alone?

How exactly will I earn my money? Who will be paying me for my work?

How much might I earn?

Who do I know that already works at something like this?

I would encourage you to talk to people and ask them tons of questions about their work. Find out how they got their job and what kinds of things they do during their work day. Be like a newspaper or television reporter and get the inside scoop. If you don't know anyone who has the kind of job you'd like, talk to your parents or a teacher about how to get in touch with someone.

Remember, you probably won't magically win a ton of money, and I can almost guarantee that no one is going to hand you enough money to live on for the rest of your life. So put your bright and creative brain to work now by thinking about what you will do someday to earn your own living.

My Kind of Work

Grab a few old magazines and cut out pictures of girls and women doing the kinds of work that you think would be really interesting and fun. Glue the pictures you have chosen onto this page to remind you of all the fun things you can do now as a girl or later as a grown woman to earn money and enjoy your work day. Have fun!

SAY *What?*

Words you may not know (but now you do!):

Checking account: An account you keep with your bank where you deposit (put in) money and write a check to buy or pay for an item.

Deposit: Adding money to a bank account.

Earning a living: Working to earn money to pay for everything you need—bills as well as fun.

Entrepreneurism: Being in charge of your own work or business. You're the boss!

Savings account: An account kept at a bank where you add (deposit) money to save.

WORD FIND

CASH	SAVINGS	FINANCES
PRICE	ENTREPRENEUR	SMART
DEPOSIT	EARN A LIVING	SHARING
WORK	ALLOWANCE	MONEY
CAREER	BUSINESS	GIRL
	CHECKING	

```
A C L P X I M V E B T C
C A S F I N A N C E S S
H S W O R G M O O N H Y
E H E C N A W O L L A A
C M D T Y D C A T T L O
K P O T Y X E A W O R K
I B E N E Q N P R E Z W
N F S R E Y J P O E O O
G R S Z T Y L H X S E T
S G N I V A S P K U I R
P R I C E X L B V E Q T
E A R N A L I V I N G !
X J H S M A R T G I R L
R U E N E R P E R T N E
T R W X B U S I N E S S
O W Z I G N I R A H S P
```

Chapter 9

Making *Dreams* Come True for REAL

Dear Brave New Girl:

I have so many dreams for when I grow up. It seems like every day I come up with new ideas. I'm smart and have lots of energy, so I know I can make them all come true. I wonder, though, if there are things I can do now to get started. After all, I figure, why wait so long? I want to get started today. Where should I start?

SIGNED,

READY TO GO

Dear Ready To Go:

You're in luck! It's really incredible—the whole world is waiting just for you! There is a special place in the world just for you, and no other girl can fill your spot. Your future is crackling with possibilities and you get to be the one to decide what to do with your life.

Daydreams: Every girl likes to daydream about what she wants to be when she grows up. It's fun to think about all the interesting things you'll get to do and the places you'll get to go. But the really important thing to realize is that you have to be the one to take the brave, adventurous steps to make your daydream come true.

Take action: Don't get stuck only daydreaming. Ask your parents and teachers to help you figure out at least one thing you can do to start moving toward making your dreams come true. To make a dream happen in real life, you have to take action. Not just any action, but steps that will get you closer to your dream, a little bit at a time.

Follow These Steps

Step One: First things first. Before you can make a dream come true, you have to know what that dream is. "I know that!" you're thinking. Good. So, it's time to say it out loud and write it down right here.

List three dreams:

1.

2.

3.

Step Two: Brainstorm. You may be wondering what on earth you can do right now to get started on something as big as "be a famous actress" or "be a doctor." You can't exactly go to New York and start a TV show or march into a hospital and start doing brain surgery. This step is about brainstorming (having you, your friends, and your family think up ideas about what you can do right now to move you toward your dream). Remember, it doesn't matter how wild and crazy the idea is right now. The point is to gather as much info and as many ideas as possible. There's no use sitting there all by yourself trying to dream up a zillion ideas. For example:

DREAM: OWN A HORSE RANCH

Action ideas for right now:
1. Go to the library and/or buy books on horses to learn everything you can about them.

2. Buy your own horse (a wild and crazy but fun idea)!

3. Take horseback riding lessons (they're expensive; you'll probably have to help pay for them—go back and reread Chapter 8).

4. Go to the state fair each summer and talk to horse owners.

5. Subscribe to a magazine about horses, and maybe even get a pen pal from the magazine.

Ask tons of people for their ideas. It's not that anyone else's ideas are better than yours, it's just that it's helpful to have a whole basketful of ideas to choose from. If you only have one idea to work with and it fizzles out and doesn't work, then you are royally stuck with nowhere to go. You have to start out all over again at ground zero. Lots of ideas mean lots of exciting options.

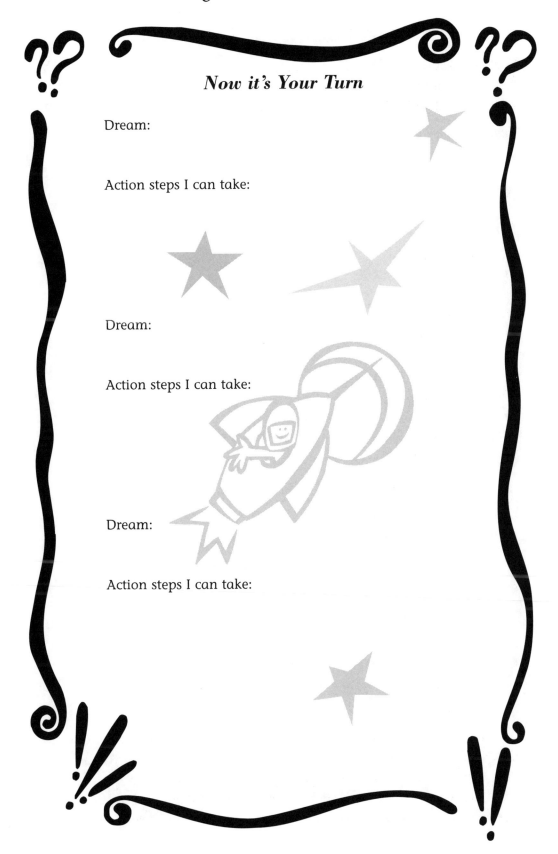

Now it's Your Turn

Dream:

Action steps I can take:

Dream:

Action steps I can take:

Dream:

Action steps I can take:

Dream Power

Check your personal "Dream Power" with the quiz below.

1. I love to daydream about what I'm going to be when I grow up:

   Yes   No

2. I even dream about it in my sleep!

   Yes   No

3. I am actively doing at least one thing in my life right now that is connected to my lifelong dream(s):

   Yes   No

4. I have met someone who actually does what I want to do:

   Yes   No

5. I have already earned money doing something I like to do:

   Yes   No

6. I have pictures on my bulletin board (door, mirror) of things that remind me of my dream:

   Yes   No

7. I have read at least one book about the subject of my dream:

   Yes   No

8. I have done at least one activity related to my dream (for example, taken a class about it, attended a camp with that theme, performed on stage, etc.):

    Yes   **No**

9. I have a plan about how to make my dream come true:

    Yes   **No**

10. My parents and friends are supportive of my dreams:

    Yes   **No**

YOUR SCORE

8–10 YES answers: Way to go! Keep planning and working on developing your dream and it will come true.

6–7 YES answers: Keep going! You're on your way.

5 or fewer YES answers: You have lots of fun times ahead of you as you start to take new action on your dreams.

HOT TIPS TO MOVE YOU TOWARD YOUR DREAM

It's so easy to procrastinate (which means to put off what you need to do until later—usually much, much later or never). The problem with procrastinating is that your dream never quite becomes reality because you keep thinking you'll start on it tomorrow, only tomorrow just comes and goes. What can you do to squash this procrastination problem?

Try to spend 10–30 minutes each day doing something, anything, that is related to your dream. (For example, if you want to be a writer, write in your journal. If you want to be forest ranger, read magazines on nature. If you think you might want to be a politician, read the daily newspaper about what's going on in the world.)

Talk about your dream every chance you get. It will keep it fresh and interesting in your mind.

Get support from others about your dream.

Go to the library and get at least one book about your topic of interest and begin reading it today.

Write a letter to someone who is doing what you want to do.

It's okay to change your dream. Just always keep dreaming and taking action on whatever dream charms you today.

Mariel's Three Ways to be Creative

1. ASK QUESTIONS. Ask yourself questions about your topic or idea.

2. TAKE YOUR IDEAS FURTHER. Expand them into something more interesting and creative.

3. THINK AND IMAGINE. Think of a bunch of ideas and turn them into one finished idea.

Mariel Shultz is currently in the fourth grade. She loves music, guinea pigs, creating minibooks, and having fun.

Here is a real treat for all you girls out there with fabulous dreams. You are now about to read three real girl stories written by three creative girls (or groups of girls) who put hard work and courage behind their dreams and turned them into reality!

Real Girl Story 1

A STORY ABOUT A STORY

BY MEGAN BROWN

I used to type on my grandpa's old typewriter back at the armory. Pressing the keys made a click, click sound.

My name is Megan Brown. I am ten years old, and in the fourth grade at Westwood Elementary School in St. Cloud, Minnesota. I have always loved to read, write, type, draw—anything to do with literature. My dream was to get my books published, and here is my story.

One day my mom and I were sitting at the table. "Mom, I want to write a book," I said. I was only in kindergarten at the time. She said, "Okay." I created a colorful character with a big nose, big stomach, and a belly button. I then tried to think of a name for the character. I remember thinking Gurbles, Werbles . . . and then BURBLES. I couldn't exactly write, so I would tell my mom what to write and she would write it down. After she had written down what I said, I would illustrate the pages.

The story became a series of stories about holidays and the creature I had made up, "Burbles." Each chapter would be about a particular holiday and Burbles. For example, *The Easter Burbles.*

Finally, the book was done. It was about forty-five pages long.

Suddenly I had an idea. What if my books were published? I had given myself a challenge. My goal and dream had then become to publish a book.

I looked in different books trying to find author's addresses. All I could find were publisher's addresses. "I guess they'll do," I thought to myself.

I then wrote to authors and illustrators asking them for advice and if they thought their publisher would publish my work. They gave me advice, but not an answer about publishing my book. Some of the authors I wrote to were Robin James, Nancy Carlson, and H.A. Rey.

Then I started to write to publishers. They didn't publish books written by young authors. Having a stack of rejection letters an inch thick did not make me feel exactly great, but I never let myself get discouraged.

My sister was practicing piano one day when I grabbed the phone book and went upstairs to my mom's room. I started calling publishers and printing presses. All of them said they didn't publish books written by children. My parents knew that I wanted to publish a book, but they didn't find out I was calling places until we got the phone bill. Ouch!

Finally, Park Press told me to call Best of Small Press in Minneapolis, Minnesota. I did that. They told me to send my work in. I did that, too. They loved the idea. They told me to write a book to introduce the character the Burbles which is now *The Rainbow Burbles,* which was published in May 1996.

My book was then published. My dream had come true. My advice to anyone and everyone is follow your dreams, love what you do, and you will achieve your goals.

Megan has now published three books: The Rainbow Burbles, The Christmas Burbles, *and* The Easter Burbles. *She is eagerly planning additional books for the future. Congratulations, Megan!*

Real Girl Story 2

WORKING ON NEW MOON MAGAZINE
BY ELIZABETH SPROAT

My name has been on the masthead of *New Moon Magazine* ever since the sample issue came out in March of 1993. Of course, the actual work started long before that. *New Moon's* first seed was sown during June of 1992. Nancy Gruver had learned that almost all girls lose their self-esteem and personal dreams between the ages of twelve and fourteen. Nancy's twin daughters Mavis and Nia were about to enter this age range, so Nancy started searching for a tool to help them through this period. She found nothing. That was when the idea of a magazine for girls first came to her. She shared the idea with her husband, Joe Kelly, who thought it was great. However, making a magazine is no easy task. They needed subscribers, a printer, and advice. They contacted other children's magazines, consultants, and friends. Still, they lacked two crucial elements: an editorial board and girls to contribute ideas. This is when the second significant idea was born: an editorial board consisting of girls ages eight to fourteen, the same age as the readers they wanted to reach. Nancy and Joe contacted the friends of Mavis and Nia. That's how I got involved. At the first editorial board meeting, there were only about ten girls, and it didn't take us long to figure out that we were the ones in charge of making the magazine. The first time that this really became clear was when we were naming *New Moon.* Nancy wanted the title to correspond to the moon, because the moon and its cycles have always been associated with women and their cycles. She had come up with Artemis, which is the name of the Greek goddess of the moon. The editorial board liked the idea of using the moon, but we hated the name Artemis. Nancy finally agreed to change the name to *New Moon.*

We worked for months deciding what departments and articles we would have, and the magazine was launched in late March 1993 when our sample issue was published. We had a big party to celebrate. We all felt really, really good to see what we had worked on for so long finally being sold in bookstores.

Being on the Girls' Editorial Board of *New Moon* includes many responsibilities. Some of them are really fun, such as going to speak at conferences and interviewing women and girls for articles. Some of them are pretty tedious, such as stuffing envelopes. However, the bulk of my duties are going to meetings where I edit and write articles, choose poems, stories, letters, and drawings to use, and share my thoughts about what *New Moon* should be. When a member turns fifteen, she has to retire because she's past the age range of our readers. However, most of the time she becomes an intern and does more "adult" work, such as helping to run meetings.

New Moon meetings are held every other Sunday from 1:30 to 4:00 P.M. During the summer, there are additional meetings on Wednesdays from 9:00 A.M. to noon. When our meetings first start, we are in a large group. We discuss issues about the magazine in general. Then we divide into smaller groups to edit individual departments or articles. When we are finished with all the material for an issue, we send it to Marian Lansky, our graphic designer. She lays out the pages and puts in graphics, borders, and other artwork. Then she sends us a rough copy. We make suggestions and write our thoughts on it. Then it's sent back to Marian to make the final corrections before being sent to the printer. A few weeks later, the end product is in our hands and the hands of girls all over the world.

New Moon Magazine *is available at most bookstores or can be ordered directly from New Moon (1-800-381-4743) or write New Moon, P.O. Box 3587, Duluth, Minnesota 55803-3587, $25.00 for one year (six issues). Here's Elizabeth Sproat working at New Moon.*

Real Girl Story 3

GIRLS OF THE U.S.A.
BY GIRL SCOUT TROOP #1562

The Beginning

It all started when our Girl Scout Troop #1562 was having its regular meeting at Glen Lake Elementary, our school in Minnetonka, Minnesota. We were in third grade at the time. Lindsay Strand, the mom of our newest troop member, came to the meeting to talk with us. She is a former television news reporter who wanted to get our input on an idea for a TV show she was developing.

Her idea was to create a show for, about, and by girls from eight to twelve years old. We were interested immediately! But instead of just giving her advice, we said we wanted to do a TV show ourselves.

The vote among troop members was unanimous. We wanted to make a show about girls, their questions, opinions, and things that interested them. We thought there should be more shows for young girls—not just teenagers and younger kids, but for us, too.

"I thought when Lindsay asked if we wanted to do a show, it was going to be taped on a home video camera and just shown back to us. Instead, it turned out that what we created was on TV, on the television news, in the newspapers, and now even in a book!" said Kathleen Waddell. "We're so young, and most of the people who do shows are adults," explained Kathleen.

Our first thought was that we were creating a TV show for the national Nickelodeon cable TV channel. (Later we settled for a spot on the local cable network—get real, right?)

At first, we thought we could put the show together in just a couple of days. But it actually took our whole school year to develop, produce, and edit. "It's a lot of work," said Scout Renee Parker.

"To be a person on TV isn't that easy. It was scary at first, but then it got easier," said Marisa Sauter.

Laura Hammer said, "We learned that girls can do really great things."

GETTING STARTED

We took action right away. At our first planning meeting, we hung a big sheet of paper from the ceiling to the floor and started brainstorming. First, we needed a name for the show. That was a challenge. Some of our ideas were "Girls are Better than Boys," "Best Friends," and "No Boys Allowed." We voted on all the names and "Girls of the U.S.A.," suggested by troop member Renee Parker, won the most votes. With the name settled, we then needed to decide what to include in our show.

Creating "Girls of the U.S.A"

Marisa Sauter liked the format she saw in girl's magazines such as *New Moon Magazine for Girls and their Dreams* and *American Girl*. She said, "A magazine format would be cool! We could share a variety of topics in an informative and entertaining format!"

Then we had to decide what to include in our show. We started to work hard on our subjects in small groups with our troop co-leaders, Alice Parker, Sue Hammer, Linda Blakesley, and Lindsay Strand.

"So many of us are involved in team sports—let's do a sports section and interview the top girls in local sports!" recommended Laura Bissonette. We looked in the newspapers and found an article about a Notre Dame soccer player who was up for top freshman soccer player of the year. She was from Minnesota, so we were able to contact her parents to arrange an interview. The other interview was with a girl who played the up-and-coming sport of girls' hockey. Her school in Apple Valley, Minnesota, had just won the girls' high school state championship.

"It goes to show that girls can be as successful and popular as boys in sports," said Britta McCloskey.

Troop member Jamie Favorite said, "I hate seeing kids getting excluded on the playground. Let's do something that helps kids handle those situations better."

"Our second segment became a skit on advice we could offer to other girls about playing cooperatively. We had to write a script that reflected how girls felt when they were excluded, and how to talk it out and deal with those hurt feelings," said Ashley Axeen. As we were going through it, we learned more about being excluded and how to handle those situations.

"This sort of exclusion goes on every day and we hope that we helped other girls learn how to stand up for themselves," said Ashley and Jamie.

Andrea Strand liked the idea of a segment on important women in history. "But it should be HERstory," said Andrea. At first we thought we might only focus on one famous Minnesota woman because we didn't think we had a lot of choices. After doing some research we learned about lots of famous Minnesota women, and then found it difficult to narrow it down to just three!

Camber Lubarski, a fan of champion ice skater Jill Trenary, interviewed Jill's mother over the phone. We decided to talk about two women from Minnesota history, Harriet Bishop, the first woman teacher in Minnesota, and Dr. Martha Ripley, the first woman doctor in Minnesota. We were inspired by the amount of hard work and dedication these women put into their careers.

We all liked the idea of giving advice about topics that interest us. "A section called 'Girl to Girl' was interesting because we could find out what is on other girls' minds," said Jessica Lehman. We all thought shooting the show at the Mall of America *(ed.: the largest indoor mall in the United States)* would give us a more diverse group of girls to talk to, so we decided to do the segment there. We wrote to the Mall and were awarded press credentials. We set up in the midst of a display for the American Girl doll collection.

When the "Girl to Girl" team was interviewing, we found lots of camera-shy girls. "What was amazing was that people thought it was cool that we were asking for questions, but then when we asked them if they wanted to be on TV, they actually said no!" said Lauren Blakesley. "Some of the questions were really easy, like, 'What do I do if someone pushes me?' But some were hard, like, 'Will I ever see my birth mother again?' That question really stumped us. We talked to our school guidance counselor to get some expert help on our responses," said Lauren.

Making Television

Of course we all had a lot of experience watching TV, but none of us had ever been involved in creating and producing a show. We had a lot to learn.

One of the first things we did was find out how the pros did it. We went to visit Channel 5 News, KSTP-TV, the local ABC affiliate. We had a behind-the-scenes tour and watched the evening news being produced. We learned some helpful hints for doing our own show. "Instead of looking down, we would need to look up at the camera," Britta McCloskey noticed after watching a professional newscast.

"It was even harder for us when we were on camera because we needed to memorize our parts while the reporters on TV had scripts that they could read," said Laura Hammer.

It was interesting to see how much makeup even the male reporters wore. For our show, before we went on the air, our parents would comb and spray our hair, but we went without makeup. At Channel 5, the anchors had a makeup artist preparing them. They always seemed to have a smile on their faces, and we tried to do the same, but it wasn't always easy.

Then we had our first visit to Paragon Cable TV studio in Hopkins, Minnesota, where the filming and editing of our show was to take place. There we met the studio coordinator, Jim Schindler, who showed us how to operate the equipment, design the set, select the music, and do all the technical aspects of creating a show. For training, Jim divided us into three groups: one in the control room, one to operate the cameras, and one to perform on the set. The control room is where you control the sound, the picture quality, and direct the production. "The control room was very interesting, but you couldn't touch a lot of stuff," said Lauren Blakesley.

Scout Katie Dickson said, "Everybody wanted to operate the cameras, so we decided to take turns."

"We got to run the cameras, learning how to zoom in and out of the picture. Wearing a head set was fun because you could hear people talking to you from the control room and you could talk back to them," said Britta McCloskey.

The set was where we acted, plus we each had a speaking part for the introduction and ending. We had to wear a small microphone called a "studio mic." When she wore the mic, Katie Dickson said she felt famous!

Many of the girls felt this way. Laura Hammer said, "The lights were hot!"

We practiced our parts at Girl Scout meetings and at home with our families. When it came to filming on the set we sometimes had to repeat our parts "over and over until we got it right," chimed in Jessica Lehman. And then there was the sports interview scheduled at the last minute because our original person canceled that day.

"We were probably nervous since it was our first time on camera," said Jamie Favorite.

"We had to be careful that we didn't trip over the cables in the control room," said Laura Bissonette.

Marisa remembered, "We had to talk loudly, clearly, and slowly. We would change the set around by rearranging the fixtures between segments. We thought this would make the show more interesting."

We all had a chance to film outside the cable studio set. There were some differences in and out of the studio. To film on location at the Minnesota History Center, the Mall of America, at a skating rink, in our school gym, and the other places we visited, the camera had to be packed up and reassembled at the filming site. This took some extra time.

Laura Hammer recalled being worried about falling down in front of the camera during the skating scene. "It was cold, so we didn't want to take many retakes." There were more things to think about and control outside the studio. We had a real audience while filming at the sites, not just our leaders and parents like in the studio.

The night of the final shoot at the studio was exciting and hard work. Everyone was really tired by the end of the evening. The girls who were not in the control room, behind the camera, or on the set were waiting for their turn in a small back room. We had to be very quiet. It wasn't too hard to wait because we were busy eating pizza and drinking pop while making posters to publicize our show at school and in the community. Lauren Blakesley remembered, "We just had to be sure we didn't have pizza faces when we went on camera or sticky hands while operating the equipment."

It took forty-two hours to edit the show from several hours of recording down to exactly twenty-nine minutes. We couldn't have done it without the technical assistance of Mike Strand, Andrea's dad, and Jim Schindler from Paragon Cable. We learned about the process by doing it, and learned that it was a lot of work!

Challenges

We knew it would be hard to learn about editing and scriptwriting. But there was other hard stuff, too. It could be hard to agree on who got in which groups. To the end, some girls still talked about not being in the segment they wanted. It was a lesson in compromise for everyone. Hauling around the equipment and assembling the equipment properly was a lot of work—there seemed to be wires and connectors everywhere! It was also difficult to find a second hockey interview when the first one canceled on the day of the interview. We called several of the families of the girls who had just won the girls' high school state hockey championship, until we finally found someone who was able to come at the last minute.

Fame and Glory

When all the hard work was done, the real fun began. The interviews and publicity increased as the show was ready to debut. We were able to convince a metropolitan cable company to air our show throughout the Twin Cities area. "The interviews were fun at first. In the end, we got so many interviews that they became no big deal," says Jessica Lehman.

We did the publicity ourselves, writing the press releases and mailing letters to reporters, anchors, and editors. Our school in Minnetonka announced the airing of the show throughout the day on the school monitors. We were featured in several newspapers and two television newscasts. "I felt so famous," says Renee Parker about the several interviews she had.

The news team from *Minnesota Nightly* from Channel 2 *(ed.: Minnesota Public Television)* came to our premier party at a co-leader's house and interviewed some of us. "It was really impressive because there were lights and cameras everywhere, following us room to room," commented Laura Bissonette.

Another exciting event was when Paragon Cable had a special awards dinner honoring people in the community who had produced a show during the year. We were the youngest people there. They had a big, long submarine sandwich with all the trimmings for dinner. They showed parts of the shows that were created by everyone and then the people who were in them came up to talk about them. We all got certificates and some of the girls won prizes from the raffle. It was another fun event that made us "feel like stars," exclaimed Kathleen Waddell.

"I really felt like someone important after an interview for the TV news," said Andrea Strand. "But the most exciting thing was when someone actually came up to me out of the blue and said she recognized me from the show!"

Now we feel more like someone, not just any regular kid. We learned that our opinions really matter. Ari Levitus, who is new to our troop this year, tells us that we seem different. "Everyone feels more confident in themselves," says Ari.

Kyley Tucker, the newest person to join our troop, was amazed at "How much the Girl Scouts learned and experienced while working on the show."

Britta said, "It's hard work and it's worth it!"

Laura Hammer felt, "It will probably be a little easier the second time."

Marisa's best advice, "Go for it!"

Renee's best advice, "You can do it if you put your mind to it."

Kathleen's best advice, "It's really fun."

Andrea's best advice, "If you have something you like to do, stick with it."

Ari's best advice, "Just stick with it."

Kyley seemed to sum up the opinion of the girls: "It was cool and radical."

Lifetime Lessons

We aren't on Nickelodeon—yet. But sometimes one dream leads you to another. You learn something you weren't expecting.We think we all feel like we accomplished a lot.

One of the things we learned was how long it really takes to put a show together (it takes longer than it looks!). It was not all fame and glory—it was a lot of work and long hours under a hot camera. We hope we got the point across that girls and boys are equal. We enjoyed all the recognition for what we did.

It also gave us an idea of what jobs there are in the TV business. Some of us like it under the lights, but others of us are more interested in what goes on behind the camera. We think some of us may end up having careers in the television business. And we are still pursuing the idea of developing this show nationally. One more thing: the boys used to exclude us from basketball during recess, but they don't anymore.

By seeing the results of what we accomplished, it got us thinking about our own personal dreams. And we're thinking BIG. Here are our dreams.

Renee's dream: "If I can't be a famous actress, I'll be president."

Ari's dream: "I want to be the president, too."

Laura H.'s dream: "I want to be an Olympic swimmer."

Kathleen's dream: "To be a veterinarian."

Katie's dream: "I want to be a veterinarian, too."

Andrea's dream: "I want to be a nurse and find a cure for cancer."

Marisa's dream: "I'm going to get a black belt in karate."

Laura B.'s dream: "To be a professional TV person, and be really good at it."

Britta's dream: "I want to own a ranch."

Ashley's dream: "I want to be a kindergarten teacher."

Jamie's dream: "I'm going to be a worldwide veterinarian."

Lauren's dream: "My dream is to be a famous soccer player and play on an international team."

Jessica's dream: "I want to be a history teacher."

Kyley's dream: "I want to be a professional basketball player."

The following girls participated in the making of "Girls of the U.S.A." All girls are from Glen Lake Elementary School, Hopkins School District, Minnetonka, Minnesota. All were between the ages of nine and ten when "Girls of the U.S.A." was produced: Ashley Axeen, Lauren Blakesley, Laura Bissonette, Ashley Buller, Katie Dickson, Jamie Favorite, Laura Hammer, Jessica Lehman, Camber Lubarski, Britta McCloskey, Renee Parker, Stephanie Pivec, Alli Saari, Marisa Sauter, Andrea Strand, Kathleen Waddell, Kelly Whittenhove.

The following girls participated in the writing of this chapter for Brave New Girls. At the time of the writing, all were between the ages of ten and eleven: Ashley Axeen, Lauren Blakesley, Laura Bissonette, Katie Dickson, Jamie Favorite, Laura Hammer, Jessica Lehman, Ari Levitus, Britta McCloskey, Renee Parker, Marisa Sauter, Andrea Strand, Kyley Tucker, Kathleen Waddell.

BE A BRAVE NEW GIRL

Chapter 10

$\mathcal{P}$UTTING It All $\mathcal{T}$ogether

You did it! You read this book and you've thought about yourself, your future, your money, your relationships, and your LIFE. Now go out and have a perfectly wonderful life and remember to take super-good care of yourself.

Check out these top ten highlights and go for it, girls!

Any thoughts, questions, or comments you want to send my way? Please feel free to contact me at:

Jeanette S. Gadeberg
c/o Brave New Girls
P.O. Box 24214
Edina, Minnesota 55424

SMART & Sassy!

1. **Opinions:** My opinion counts!

2. **Good choices:** I can make good, strong, healthy choices for my life.

3. **Getting help:** If I get super-stuck, I can ask others to help me out.

4. **Stand firm:** Sometimes I have to stand firm and make a tough decision.

5. **Compromising:** Compromising helps me get along with others.

6. **Self-talk:** "Self-talk" is important. What I tell myself matters.

7. **Affirmations:** I can learn to think positively by remembering short, positive messages called "affirmations."

8. **Herstory:** I can write down my own life story in a diary or journal.

9. **Courage:** Even if I'm scared, I can still be brave.

10. **Fairness:** I can choose to be fair and open-minded. People will like me more if I am.

One thing I'm going to do from now on to express my opinion will be to:

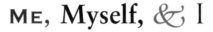

ME, Myself, & I

1. **Changing feelings:** My feelings are changing a lot right now, and that's okay.

2. **Naming feelings:** It helps to name my feelings and talk to someone about them.

3. **Bad moods:** Sometimes I'm in a seriously bad mood, but I'm still loveable.

4. **Fear busters:** Taking action helps my worries and fears go away. I never have to be alone with my fears. I can always talk to someone.

5. **Taking charge:** There are some actions I can take to help me feel more in charge of my life.

6. **Being brave:** I can work toward bravery, but it's okay to wimp out sometimes.

7. **What is normal:** Normal? Who, me? Who knows! But I like myself anyway.

8. **Hurt feelings:** I have to remember to tell people when they hurt my feelings, so I don't walk around feeling lousy all day.

9. **Anger:** I need to admit when I'm angry and let the other person know in a positive, non-hurtful way.

10. **Growing my own happiness:** My happiness is up to me. No one else is responsible for making me happy—that's my job.

Starting today, I will remember how important my feelings are. Here is who I will tell my feelings to today:

Friends FOREVER

1. **New friends:** I can be a friend to a new girl. I know I'd like someone to do the same for me.

2. **Ups and downs:** If one of my friendships is on the rocks, I can still act friendly toward the person while also staying connected to my other friends.

3. **Fair and square:** Everyone sees the world a little differently. I can accept that.

4. **Staying friends:** There are tons of things I can do to be a really good friend. Others will love me for it, too.

5. **Being positive:** If I choose to see the good instead of the bad, people will want to hang out with me.

6. **Jealousy:** Everyone gets jealous sometimes. I can focus on what's good in my life to help cheer me up.

7. **Negative talk:** Who needs it? Everyone feels bad sometimes, but as much as I can, I choose to have a sunny attitude and a smile on my face.

8. **Worrying about my friends:** If my friend is heading off in a dumb direction, I can tell her I'm worried about her, or tell an adult, but I can't control her life.

9. **Keep my own nose clean:** I can make good decisions and don't need to follow anyone else's bad idea.

10. **Boys:** They're cool. But for now, let's just be friends.

Beginning this very moment, I will be a better friend by:

Getting It **ALL DONE**

1. **My style:** Everyone has their own style of how to get things done.

2. **Feeling overwhelmed:** I can break a big project down into bite-sized pieces, or ask for help.

3. **Studying:** I can make a list of ten ways to study for quizzes and tests and check off each one as I do it.

4. **Organizing projects:** If I do a little bit on a big project every day, I won't have to hide in the closet when it's due.

5. **Time eaters:** I am going to take an honest look at the junk stuff that I do that eats up my time.

6. **The queen's castle:** All right, it's time to do a serious, blow-out cleaning of my room. I will throw out or give away anything I don't truly need or want.

7. **Stress busters:** I don't have to get everything done perfectly, or even do my best all the time. I need to remind myself to relax.

8. **Doing what I can:** All I really need to do, is what I am able to do at any given moment.

9. **Relax—time out:** Every day I'm going to do at least one thing that I really want to do—something that helps me feel really good and happy.

10. **Phooey on perfectionism:** I do NOT have to be perfect! I'm absolutely wonderful just the way I am.

I can get seriously organized by doing this one thing every single day:

It's a BiG WoRLd OuT tHERe

1. **Helping out:** I will take action to make this world a better place.

2. **Working with friends:** My friends and I can work together to help others and clean up Mother Earth.

3. **Joining up:** I can join up, make noise, and get involved!

4. **Heads and hands:** I will learn how to do at least one new thing around the house, where I have to use my head and my hands.

5. **Mechanical stuff:** Handling machines and household items isn't just for boys. I am perfectly capable of learning how to do it myself.

6. **Buzzing around:** I need to learn how to get around without getting lost.

7. **Getting lost:** I have a plan for what to do whenever I find myself completely lost.

8. **Cultural diversity:** Everyone is so different. Isn't that just wonderful?

9. **Home sweet home:** I really feel like I belong.

10. **My heritage:** I want to learn everything I can about my cultural background. It's important. It's a huge part of who I am.

To help me learn my way around the next time I go someplace, I will:

My Family & Me

1. **Tales of the weird:** I'm stuck with my goofy family, so I'd better find a way to live happily with them.

2. **Privacy zones:** I have a right to my privacy. Nobody should barge in on me, read my private stuff, or listen to my conversations.

3. **Ground rules:** It helps to have ground rules that my siblings and I have to follow to live peacefully in our house.

4. **Siblings:** They're the best and the worst. Of course, the better I treat them, the better they treat me.

5. **Not so many no's:** I can think through how to talk to my parents, so maybe they won't say no so often.

6. **My own ideas about rules:** I could write down my own ideas about household rules and then request a family meeting to talk about them.

7. **Life is a "we thing":** Isn't it great that I don't have to do this thing called life alone? I can ask for help anytime I want.

8. **Not fair!:** Sometimes life in a family doesn't feel fair.

9. **Family fun:** It might actually be possible to enjoy being with my family.

10. **Getting yelled at:** There are some wonderful sure-fire ways to get yelled at, if I want to.

I promise that I will try to be easier to live with. One thing I will do is:

"Hey, *That's* NOT FAIR!"

1. **The media:** I need to decide for myself what's right and wrong.

2. **The real world vs. the media:** The real world is different from the fantasy I see on TV or in the movies.

3. **Action plan:** I can write a letter to express my true feelings about TV shows and movies.

4. **Movies:** Lots of movies are filled with violence toward women. What do I think about it?

5. **Advertisements:** Advertisers want me to spend money on their products. What do I want to do?

6. **Clothes:** Clothes are so cool and so expensive. Do I need special clothes to feel good about myself?

7. **Girlcott the junk:** I can avoid products I see advertised. The advertisers are saying that buying their product will make me better. Get real! I'm great just the way I am.

8. **Harassment:** If anyone is bothering me, I promise to tell an adult. I deserve to be treated well.

9. **Hurtful relationships:** If a "friend" keeps hurting my feelings, I may need to decide if we can still be friends. I can find other friends who won't hurt me.

10. **Rumors:** I promise not to spread rumors. They hurt.

If I see yucky stuff in the media, I will write a letter and express my opinion. I will watch for: